3,50
X

A NIGHT OUT
NIGHT SCHOOL
REVUE SKETCHES

2.40

⊆

Previously Published

# A NIGHT OUT
# NIGHT SCHOOL
# REVUE SKETCHES

Early Plays

*by* Harold Pinter

Grove Press, Inc., New York

Library of Congress Catalog Card Number: 68-54860
Second Printing
Manufactured in the United States of America

# A NIGHT OUT

*A Night Out* was first performed on the B.B.C. Third Programme on 1 March 1960, with the following cast:

| | |
|---|---|
| ALBERT STOKES | Barry Foster |
| MRS. STOKES, *his mother* | Mary O'Farrell |
| SEELEY | Harold Pinter |
| KEDGE | John Rye |
| BARMAN AT THE COFFEE STALL | Walter Hall |
| OLD MAN | Norman Wynne |
| MR. KING | David Bird |
| MR. RYAN | Norman Wynne |
| GIDNEY | Nicholas Selby |
| JOYCE | Jane Jordan Rogers |
| EILEEN | Auriol Smith |
| BETTY | Margaret Hotine |
| HORNE | Hugh Dickson |
| BARROW | David Spenser |
| THE GIRL | Vivien Merchant |

Produced by Donald McWhinnie

The play was televised by A.B.C. Armchair Theatre on 24 April 1960, with the following cast:

| | |
|---|---|
| ALBERT STOKES | Tom Bell |
| MRS. STOKES, *his mother* | Madge Ryan |
| SEELEY | Harold Pinter |
| KEDGE | Philip Locke |
| BARMAN AT THE COFFEE STALL | Edmond Bennett |
| OLD MAN | Gordon Phillott |
| MR. KING | Arthur Lowe |
| MR. RYAN | Edward Malin |
| GIDNEY | Stanley Meadows |
| JOYCE | José Read |
| EILEEN | Maria Lennard |
| BETTY | Mary Duddy |
| HORNE | Stanley Segal |
| BARROW | Walter Hall |
| THE GIRL | Vivien Merchant |

Produced by Philip Saville

# Act One

*SCENE ONE*

*The kitchen of* MRS. STOKES' *small house in the south of London. Clean and tidy.*

ALBERT, *a young man of twenty-eight, is standing in his shirt and trousers, combing his hair in the kitchen mirror over the mantelpiece. A woman's voice calls his name from upstairs. He ignores it, picks up a brush from the mantelpiece and brushes his hair. The voice calls again. He slips the comb in his pocket, bends down, reaches under the sink and takes out a shoe duster. He begins to polish his shoes.* MRS. STOKES *descends the stairs, passes through the hall and enters the kitchen.*

MOTHER: Albert, I've been calling you. [*She watches him.*] What are you doing?

ALBERT: Nothing.

MOTHER: Didn't you hear me call you, Albert? I've been calling you from upstairs.

ALBERT: You seen my tie?

MOTHER: Oh, I say, I'll have to put the flag out.

ALBERT: What do you mean?

MOTHER: Cleaning your shoes? I'll have to put the flag out, won't I?

ALBERT *puts the brush back under the sink and begins to search the sideboard and cupboard.*

What are you looking for?

ALBERT: My tie. The striped one, the blue one.

MOTHER: The bulb's gone in Grandma's room.

ALBERT: Has it?

MOTHER: That's what I was calling you about. I went in and switched on the light and the bulb had gone.

*She watches him open the kitchen cabinet and look into it.*

Aren't those your best trousers, Albert? What have you put on your best trousers for?

ALBERT: Look, Mum, where's my tie? The blue one, the blue tie, where is it? You know the one I mean, the blue striped one, I gave it to you this morning.

MOTHER: What do you want your tie for?

ALBERT: I want to put it on. I asked you to press it for me this morning. I gave it to you this morning before I went to work, didn't I?

*She goes to the gas stove, examines the vegetables, opens the oven and looks into it.*

MOTHER: Well, your dinner'll be ready soon. You can look for it afterwards. Lay the table, there's a good boy.

ALBERT: Why should I look for it afterwards? You know where it is now.

MOTHER: You've got five minutes. Go down to the cellar, Albert, get a bulb and put it in Grandma's room, go on.

ALBERT: I don't know why you keep calling that room Grandma's room, she's been dead ten years.

MOTHER: Albert!

ALBERT: I mean, it's just a junk room, that's all it is.

MOTHER: Albert, that's no way to speak about your Grandma, you know that as well as I do.

ALBERT: I'm not saying a word against Grandma—

MOTHER: You'll upset me in a minute, you go on like that.

ALBERT: I'm not going on about anything.

MOTHER: Yes, you are. Now why don't you go and put a bulb in Grandma's room and by the time you come down I'll have your dinner on the table.

ALBERT: I can't go down to the cellar, I've got my best trousers on, I've got a white shirt on.

MOTHER: You're dressing up tonight, aren't you? Dressing up, cleaning your shoes, anyone would think you were going to the Ritz.

ALBERT: I'm not going to the Ritz.

MOTHER: What do you mean, you're not going to the Ritz?

ALBERT: What do you mean?

MOTHER: The way you said you're not going to the Ritz, it sounded like you were going somewhere else.

ALBERT [*wearily*]: I am.

MOTHER [*shocked surprise*]: You're going out?

ALBERT: You know I'm going out. I told you I was going out. I told you last week. I told you this morning. Look, where's my tie? I've got to have my tie. I'm late already. Come on, Mum, where'd you put it?

MOTHER: What about your dinner?

ALBERT [*searching*]: Look . . . I told you . . . I haven't got the . . . wait a minute . . . ah, here it is.

MOTHER: You can't wear that tie. I haven't pressed it.

ALBERT: You have. Look at it. Of course you have. It's beautifully pressed. It's fine.


*He ties the tie.*

MOTHER: Where are you going?

ALBERT: Mum, I've told you, honestly, three times. Honestly, I've told you three times I had to go out tonight.

MOTHER: No, you didn't.

ALBERT *exclaims and knots the tie.*

I thought you were joking.

ALBERT: I'm not going . . . I'm just going to Mr. King's. I've told you. You don't believe me.

MOTHER: You're going to Mr. King's?

ALBERT: Mr. Ryan's leaving. You know Ryan. He's leaving the firm. He's been there years. So Mr. King's giving a sort of party for him at his house . . . well, not exactly a party, not a party, just a few . . . you know . . . anyway, we're all invited. I've got to go. Everyone else is going. I've got to go. I don't want to go, but I've got to.

MOTHER [*bewildered, sitting*]: Well, I don't know . . .

ALBERT [*with his arm round her*]: I won't be late. I don't want to go. I'd much rather stay with you.

MOTHER: Would you?

ALBERT: You know I would. Who wants to go to Mr. King's party?

MOTHER: We were going to have our game of cards.

ALBERT: Well, we can't have our game of cards.

[*Pause.*]

MOTHER: Put the bulb in Grandma's room, Albert.

ALBERT: I've told you I'm not going down to the cellar in my white shirt. There's no light in the cellar either. I'll be pitch black in five minutes, looking for those bulbs.

MOTHER: I told you to put a light in the cellar. I told you yesterday.

ALBERT: Well, I can't do it now.

MOTHER: If we had a light in the cellar you'd be able to see where those bulbs were. You don't expect me to go down to the cellar?

ALBERT: I don't know why we keep bulbs in the cellar!

[*Pause.*]

MOTHER: Your father would turn in his grave if he heard you raise your voice to me. You're all I've got, Albert. I want you to remember that. I haven't got anyone else. I want you . . . I want you to bear that in mind.

ALBERT: I'm sorry . . . I raised my voice.

*He goes to the door.*

[*Mumbling.*] I've got to go.

MOTHER [*following*]: Albert!

ALBERT: What?

MOTHER: I want to ask you a question.

ALBERT: What?

MOTHER: Are you leading a clean life?

ALBERT: A clean life?

MOTHER: You're not leading an unclean life, are you?

ALBERT: What are you talking about?

MOTHER: You're not messing about with girls, are you? You're not going to go messing about with girls tonight?

ALBERT: Don't be so ridiculous.

MOTHER: Answer me, Albert. I'm your mother.

ALBERT: I don't know any girls.

MOTHER: If you're going to the firm's party, there'll be girls there, won't there? Girls from the office?

ALBERT: I don't like them, any of them.

MOTHER: You promise?

ALBERT: Promise what?

MOTHER: That . . . that you won't upset your father.

ALBERT: My father? How can I upset my father? You're always talking about upsetting people who are dead!

MOTHER: Oh, Albert, you don't know how you hurt me, you don't know the hurtful way you've got, speaking of your poor father like that.

ALBERT: But he is dead.

MOTHER: He's not! He's living! [*Touching her breast.*] In here! And this is his house!

[*Pause.*]

ALBERT: Look, Mum, I won't be late . . . and I won't . . .

MOTHER: But what about your dinner? It's nearly ready.

ALBERT: Seeley and Kedge are waiting for me. I told you not to cook dinner this morning. [*He goes to the stairs.*] Just because you never listen . . .

*He runs up the stairs and disappears. She calls after him from the hall.*

MOTHER: Well, what am I going to do while you're out? I can't go into Grandma's room because there's no light. I can't go down to the cellar in the dark, we were going to have a game of cards, it's Friday night, what about our game of rummy?

## SCENE TWO

*A coffee stall by a railway arch. A wooden bench is situated a short distance from it.*

SEELEY *and* KEDGE, *both about* ALBERT'S *age, are at the counter, talking to the barman. An old man leans at the corner of the counter.*

SEELEY: Give us a cheese roll as well, will you?

KEDGE: Make it two.

SEELEY: Make it two.

BARMAN: Two cheese rolls.

SEELEY: What are these, sausages?

BARMAN: Best pork sausages.

SEELEY [*to* KEDGE]: You want a sausage?

KEDGE [*shuddering*]: No, thanks.

SEELEY: Yes, you're right.

BARMAN: Two cheese rolls. What about these sausages, you want them or don't you?

SEELEY: Just the rolls, mate.

BARMAN: Two tea, two rolls, makes one and eightpence.

SEELEY *gives him half a crown.*

KEDGE: There'll be plenty to eat at the party.

SEELEY: I'll bet.

OLD MAN: Eh! [*They turn to him.*] Your mate was by here not long ago.

SEELEY: Which mate?

OLD MAN: He had a cup of tea, didn't he, Fred? Sitting over there he was, on the bench. He said he was going home to change but to tell you he'd be back.

KEDGE: Uh-uh.

OLD MAN: Not gone more than above forty-five minutes.

BARMAN: One and eight from half a dollar leaves you ten pennies.

OLD MAN: Anyway, he told me to tell you when I see you he was coming back.

KEDGE: Thanks very much.

SEELEY: Well, I hope he won't be long. I don't want to miss the booze.

KEDGE: You think there'll be much there, do you?

OLD MAN: Yes, he was sitting over there.

KEDGE: Who was?

OLD MAN: Your mate.

SEELEY: Oh yes.

OLD MAN: Yes, sitting over there he was. Took his cup of tea and went and sat down, didn't he, Fred? He sat there looking very compressed with himself.

KEDGE: Very what?

OLD MAN: Compressed. I thought he was looking compressed, didn't you, Fred?

BARMAN: Depressed. He means depressed.

SEELEY: No wonder. What about that game on Saturday, eh?

KEDGE: You were going to tell me. You haven't told me yet.

BARMAN: What game? Fulham?

SEELEY: No, the firm. Firm's got a team, see? Play on Saturdays.

BARMAN: Who'd you play?

SEELEY: Other firms.

BARMAN: You boys in the team, are you?

KEDGE: Yes. I've been off sick though. I didn't play last week.

BARMAN: Sick, eh? You want to try one of my sausages, don't he, Henry?

OLD MAN: Oh, ay, yes.

KEDGE: What happened with the game, then?

*They move to the bench.*

SEELEY: Well, when you couldn't play, Gidney moved Albert to left back.

KEDGE: He's a left half.

SEELEY: I know he's a left half. I said to Gidney myself, I said to him, look, why don't you go left back, Gidney? He said, no, I'm too valuable at centre half.

KEDGE: He didn't, did he?

SEELEY: Yes. Well, you know who was on the right wing, don't you? Connor.

KEDGE: Who? Tony Connor?

SEELEY: No. You know Connor. What's the matter with you? You've played against Connor yourself.

KEDGE: Oh—whatsisname—Micky Connor.

SEELEY: Yes.

KEDGE: I thought he'd given up the game.

SEELEY: No, what are you talking about? He plays for the printing works, plays outside right for the printing works.

KEDGE: He's a good ballplayer, that Connor, isn't he?

SEELEY: Look. I said to Albert before the kick off, Connor's on the right wing, I said, play your normal game. I told him six times before the kick off.

KEDGE: What's the good of him playing his normal game? He's a left half, he's not a left back.

SEELEY: Yes, but he's a defensive left half, isn't he? That's why I told him to play his normal game. You don't want to worry about Connor, I said, he's a good ballplayer but he's not all that good.

KEDGE: Oh, he's good, though.

SEELEY: No one's denying he's good. But he's not all that good. I mean, he's not tip-top. You know what I mean?

KEDGE: He's fast.

SEELEY: He's fast, but he's not all that fast, is he?

KEDGE [*doubtfully*]: Well, not all that fast . . .

SEELEY: What about Levy? Was Levy fast?

KEDGE: Well, Levy was a sprinter.

SEELEY: He was a dasher, Levy. All he knew was run.

KEDGE: He could move.

SEELEY: Yes, but look how Albert played him! He cut him off, he played him out the game. And Levy's faster than Connor.

KEDGE: Yes, but he wasn't so clever, though.

SEELEY: Well, what about Foxall?

KEDGE: Who? Lou Foxall?

SEELEY: No, you're talking about Lou Fox, I'm talking about Sandy Foxall.

KEDGE: Oh, the winger.

SEELEY: Sure. He was a very smart ballplayer, Foxall. But what did Albert do? He played his normal game. He let him come. He waited for him. And Connor's not as clever as Foxall.

KEDGE: He's clever though.

SEELEY: Gawd blimey, I know he's clever, but he's not as clever as Foxall, is he?

KEDGE: The trouble is, with Connor, he's fast too, isn't he?

SEELEY: But if Albert would have played his normal game! He played a game foreign to him.

KEDGE: How many'd Connor get?

SEELEY: He made three and scored two.

*Pause. They eat.*

KEDGE: No wonder he's depressed, old Albert.

SEELEY: Oh, he was very depressed after the game, I can tell you. And of course Gidney was after him, of course. You know Gidney.

KEDGE: That birk.

[*Pause.*]

OLD MAN: Yes, he was sitting over where you are now, wasn't he, Fred? Looking very compressed with himself. Light-haired bloke, ain't he?

SEELEY: Yes, light-haired.

## SCENE THREE

*The house.*

ALBERT *is coming down the stairs. He is wearing his jacket. He goes towards the door. His mother calls from the kitchen and goes into the hall.*

MOTHER: Albert! Where are you going?

ALBERT: Out.

MOTHER: Your dinner's ready.

ALBERT: I'm sorry. I haven't got time to have it.

MOTHER: Look at your suit. You're not going out with your suit in that state, are you?

ALBERT: What's the matter with it?

MOTHER: It needs a good brush, that's what's the matter with it. You can't go out like that. Come on, come in here and I'll give it a brush.

ALBERT: It's all right . . .

MOTHER: Come on.

*They go into the kitchen. She gets the brush.*

Turn round. No, stand still. You can't go out and disgrace me, Albert. If you've got to go out you've got to look nice. There, that's better.

*She dusts his jacket with her hands and straightens his tie.*

I didn't tell you what I made for you, did I? I made it specially. I made Shepherd's Pie tonight.

ALBERT [*taking her hand from his tie*]: The tie's all right.

*He goes to the door.*

Well, ta-ta.

MOTHER: Albert! Wait a minute. Where's your handkerchief?

ALBERT: What handkerchief?

MOTHER: You haven't got a handkerchief in your breast pocket.

ALBERT: That doesn't matter, does it?

MOTHER: Doesn't matter? I should say it does matter. Just a minute. [*She takes a handkerchief from a drawer.*] Here you are. A nice clean one. [*She arranges it in his pocket.*] You mustn't let me down, you know. You've got to be properly dressed. Your father was always properly dressed. You'd never see him out without a handkerchief in his breast pocket. He always looked like a gentleman.


## SCENE FOUR

*The coffee stall.*
KEDGE *is returning from the counter with two teas.*


KEDGE: Time we were there.

SEELEY: We'll give him five minutes.

KEDGE: I bet his Mum's combing his hair for him, eh?

*He chuckles and sits.*

You ever met her, Seeley?

SEELEY: Who?

KEDGE: His . . . mother.

SEELEY: Yes.

KEDGE: What's she like?

SEELEY [*shortly*]: She's all right.

KEDGE: All right, is she?

SEELEY: I told you. I just said she was all right.

[*Pause.*]

KEDGE: No, what I mean is, he always gets a bit niggly when she's mentioned, doesn't he? A bit touchy. You noticed that?

SEELEY [*unwillingly*]: Yes.

KEDGE: Why's that, then?

SEELEY: I don't know. What're you asking me for?

KEDGE: I don't know. I just thought you might . . . sort of . . . well, I mean, you know him better than I do, don't you? [*Pause.*]

Of course, he don't let much slip, does he, old Albert?

SEELEY: No, not much.

KEDGE: He's a bit deep really, isn't he?

SEELEY: Yes, he's a bit deep.

[*Pause.*]

KEDGE: Secretive.

SEELEY [*irritably*]: What do you mean, secretive? What are you talking about?

KEDGE: I was just saying he was secretive.

SEELEY: What are you talking about? What do you mean, he's secretive?

KEDGE: You said yourself he was deep.

SEELEY: I said he was deep. I didn't say he was secretive!

ALBERT *walks through the railway arch across to the bench.*

KEDGE: Hullo, Albert.

ALBERT: Hullo.

KEDGE: That's a nice bit of clobber you've got on there.

SEELEY: Very fair, very fair.

KEDGE: Yes, fits you like a glove.

SEELEY: Well, come on.

ALBERT: Wait a minute, I . . . I don't think I feel like going, actually.

KEDGE: What are you talking about?

ALBERT: I don't feel like it, that's all.

SEELEY: What, with all that drink laid on?

ALBERT: No, I've just got a bit of a headache.

OLD MAN: That's the bloke! That's the bloke was here before, isn't it, Fred? I gave them your message, son.

ALBERT: Oh . . . thanks.

OLD MAN: Didn't I?

KEDGE: You did, you did, mate.

SEELEY: Well, what's going on, you coming or what?

ALBERT: No, I feel a bit . . . you know . . .        t . . . you

KEDGE: Don't you know who'll be there tonight, Albert?

ALBERT: Who?

KEDGE: Joyce.

ALBERT: Joyce? Well, what about it?

KEDGE: And Eileen.

ALBERT: Well, so what?

KEDGE: And Betty. Betty'll be there. They'll all be there.

SEELEY: Betty? Who's Betty?

KEDGE: Betty? What do you mean? You don't know Betty?

SEELEY: There's no girl in the office called Betty.

KEDGE: Betty! The dark bit! The new one. The one that came in last week. The little one, in the corner!

SEELEY: Oh, her. Is her name Betty? I thought it was—

KEDGE: Betty. Her name's Betty.

SEELEY: I've been calling her Hetty.

[Pause.]

KEDGE: Anywhat, she'll be there. She's raring to go, that one.

ALBERT: Well, you go then, I'll . . .

KEDGE: Albert, what's the matter with you, mate? It's wine, women and song tonight.

ALBERT: I see them every day, don't I? What's new in that?

KEDGE: You frightened Gidney'll be after you, then, because of the game?

ALBERT: What do you mean?

KEDGE: Go on, everyone has a bad game, Albert.

ALBERT: Yes, they do, don't they?

KEDGE: I played against Connor myself once. He's tricky. He's a very tricky ballplayer.

ALBERT: Yes.

SEELEY: Clever player, Connor.

ALBERT: What's Gidney got to do with it, Kedge?

KEDGE: Well, you know what he is.

ALBERT: What?

KEDGE: Well, he's captain of the team, isn't he, for a bang-off?

ALBERT: You think—?

SEELEY: Oh, scrub round it, will you? It's late—

ALBERT: You think I'm frightened of Gidney?

KEDGE: I didn't say you were—

SEELEY: Gidney's all right. What's the matter with Gidney?

ALBERT: Yes. What's wrong with him?

KEDGE: Nothing. There's nothing wrong with him. He's a nice bloke. He's a charmer, isn't he?

SEELEY: The cream of the cream. Well, come on, you coming or what?

ALBERT: Yes, all right. I'll come.

SEELEY: Just a minute. I'll get some fags.

*He goes to the counter.* ALBERT *and* KEDGE *are left standing.*

[*To the* BARMAN.] Twenty 'Weights', mate.

KEDGE *regards* ALBERT.

KEDGE: How's your Mum, Albert?

ALBERT: All right.

KEDGE: That's the idea.

BARMAN: Only got 'Woods'.

SEELEY: They'll do.

ALBERT [*quietly*]: What do you mean, how's my Mum?

KEDGE: I just asked how she was, that's all.

ALBERT: Why shouldn't she be all right?

KEDGE: I didn't say she wasn't.

ALBERT: Well, she is.

KEDGE: Well, that's all right then, isn't it?

ALBERT: What are you getting at?

KEDGE: I don't know what's the matter with you tonight, Albert.

SEELEY [*returning*]: What's up now?

ALBERT: Kedge here, suddenly asks how my mother is.

KEDGE: Just a friendly question, that's all. Gaw! You can't even ask a bloke how his mother is now without him getting niggly!

ALBERT: Well, why's he suddenly ask—?

SEELEY: He was just asking a friendly question, mate. What's the matter with you?

[*Pause.*]

ALBERT: Oh.

SEELEY: Well, how is she, then?

ALBERT: She's fine. What about yours?

SEELEY: Fine. Fine.

[*Pause.*]

KEDGE: Mine's fine too, you know. Great. Absolutely great. A marvel for her age, my mother is. Of course, she had me very late.

[*Pause.*]

SEELEY: Well? Are you coming or not? Or what?

KEDGE: I'm coming.

ALBERT [*following*]: I'm coming.


## SCENE FIVE


*The kitchen. The* MOTHER *is putting* ALBERT'S *dinner into the oven. She takes the alarm clock from the mantelpiece and puts it on the table. She takes out a pack of cards, sits at the table and begins to lay out a game of patience. Close up of her, broodingly setting out the cards. Close up of the clock. It is seven forty-five.*

# Act Two

## SCENE ONE

*The lounge of* MR. KING'S *house. The party is in progress.* KEDGE *and* BETTY *are dancing. Music comes from a radiogram.* MR. KING, *an urbane man in his fifties,* GIDNEY, *the chief accountant, in his late twenties,* SEELEY *and* ALBERT, *are standing in a group.* JOYCE *and* EILEEN *are at the table which serves as a bar. Two men and a woman of indeterminate age sit holding drinks.* HORNE *and* BARROW, *two young clerks, stand by the door.* MR. RYAN, *the old man, sits in the centre of the room, smiling.*

JOYCE: You enjoying the party, Mr. Ryan?

RYAN *nods and smiles.*

EILEEN [*pleasantly*]: Enjoying the party, are you?

*He nods, winks and smiles.*

KING: I recommend a bicycle, honestly. It really keeps you up to the mark. Out in the morning, on the bike, through the town . . . the air in your lungs, muscles working . . . you arrive at work . . . you arrive at work fresh . . . you know what I mean? Uplifted.

GIDNEY: Not so good in the rain.

KING: Refreshes you! Clears the cobwebs. [*He laughs.*]

SEELEY: You don't walk to work, do you, Gidney?

GIDNEY: Me? I've got the car.

KING: I drive too, of course, but I often think seriously of taking up cycling again. I often think very seriously about it, you know.

JOYCE [*to* RYAN]: Nice party, isn't it, Mr. Ryan?

RYAN *nods and inclines his head, smiling.*

KEDGE [*dancing*]: You dance like a dream, Betty, you know that?

BETTY [*shyly*]: I don't.

KEDGE: You do. Honest. Like a dream. Like a dream come true.

BETTY: You're just saying that.

KING: Well, Kedge looks all right again, doesn't he? What was the matter with him? I've forgotten.

SEELEY: Stomach trouble.

KING: Not enough exercise. [*To* KEDGE.] You'll have to see you get more exercise, Kedge!

KEDGE [*passing*]: You never said a truer word, Mr. King.

SEELEY: Well, he don't look in bad trim to me, Mr. King.

*They laugh.*

KING: I must admit it.

GIDNEY: He'll never get to the last lap with that one, I can tell you.

KING [*smiling*]: Now, now, you young men, that's quite enough of that. No more of that.

GIDNEY [*pleasantly*]: What are you laughing at, Stokes?

ALBERT: What?

GIDNEY: Sorry. I thought you were laughing.

ALBERT: I was laughing. You made a joke.

GIDNEY: Oh yes, of course. Sorry.

[*Pause.*]

Well, we've got Kedge back at left back next Saturday.

KING: Yes. Excuse me.

SEELEY: That's a lovely pair of shoes you're wearing, Gidney.

GIDNEY: Do you think so?

SEELEY: Oh, they're the best, the very best, aren't they, Albert? Gidney always wears a nice pair of shoes, doesn't he, you noticed that? That's one thing I'll say about you, Gidney—you carry your feet well.

EILEEN: A mambo! Who's going to dance?

SEELEY: I'll give it a trot.

SEELEY *and* EILEEN *dance.*

GIDNEY: Don't you dance, Stokes?

ALBERT: Yes, sometimes.

GIDNEY: Do you? You will excuse me, won't you?

ALBERT: Yes.

ALBERT *is left standing.*

KING: Well, Ryan, enjoying the party?

RYAN *nods, smiles.*

Nice to see a lot of young people enjoying themselves, eh?

RYAN *nods, smiles.*

Of course, it's all in your honour, old man. Let's fill you up. I'll be the oldest man in the office after you've gone.

GIDNEY *and* JOYCE, *whispering.*

JOYCE: No. Why should I?

GIDNEY: Go on. Just for a lark.

JOYCE: What for?

GIDNEY: For a lark. Just for a lark.

JOYCE: You've got an evil mind, you have.

GIDNEY: No, it'll amuse me, that's all. I feel like being amused.

JOYCE: Well, I'm not going to.

GIDNEY: Gah, you wouldn't know how to, anyway.

JOYCE: Oh, wouldn't I?

GIDNEY [*taking her arm*]: Get hold of Eileen, don't tell her I told you though, and go over and lead him a dance, just lead him a dance, that's all, see what he does. I want to see his reaction, that's all, I just want to see how he takes it.

JOYCE: What, in front of everyone else, in front of—?

GIDNEY: Just talk to him, talk to him. I don't mean anything else, do I?

JOYCE: What do I get if I do?

GIDNEY: A toffee apple.

JOYCE: Oh, really? Thank you.

GIDNEY: I'll take you for a ride in the car. Honest.

SEELEY [*dancing*]: Hullo, Mr. Ryan. Enjoying the party?

EILEEN: You dance well, don't you?

SEELEY: I was going in for ballet once.

EILEEN: Go on!

SEELEY: Yes, true. They offered me the leading part in *Rigoletto*. When I was a boy soprano.

EILEEN: You're making it up.

GIDNEY [*to* JOYCE]: No, he just irritates me, that bloke. I . . . I haven't got any time for a bloke like that.

JOYCE: He's just quiet, that's all.

GIDNEY: Well, see if you can wake him up.

KING [*to* BETTY]: Well, Miss Todd, it hasn't taken you long to get to know everyone, has it?

BETTY: Oh no, Mr. King.

KEDGE: I've taken her under my wing, Mr. King.

KING: So I noticed.

KEDGE: Yes, I've been teaching her all about mortality tables. I told her in case of fire or burglary commission and damages come to her.

KING: I would hardly take Kedge's word as gospel, Miss Todd.

KEDGE: You know I've got the best interests of the firm at heart, Mr. King.

GIDNEY [*drinking, with* JOYCE]: Anyway, I'm thinking of moving on. You stay too long in a place you go daft. After all, with my qualifications I could go anywhere.

*He sees* ALBERT *at the bar.*

Couldn't I, Stokes?

ALBERT: What?

GIDNEY: I was saying, with my qualifications I could go anywhere. I could go anywhere and be anything.

ALBERT: So could I.

GIDNEY: Could you? What qualifications have you got?

ALBERT: Well, I've got a few, you know.

GIDNEY: Listen! Do you know that Chelsea wanted to sign me up a few years ago? They had a scout down to one of our games. They wanted to sign me up. And I'll tell you another thing as well. I could turn professional cricketer any day I wanted to, if I wanted to.

ALBERT: Then why don't you?

GIDNEY: I don't want to.

JOYCE: You'd look lovely in white.

GIDNEY: These people who talk about qualifications. Just makes me laugh, that's all.

KEDGE [*in the corner of the room, in an armchair with* BETTY]: Oh, you're lovely. You're the loveliest thing on four wheels.

KING [*to* HORNE *and* BARROW, *by the door*]: Well, I hope you'll both be in the team soon yourselves. I think it's a very good thing we've . . . that the firm's got a football team. And a cricket team, of course. It shows we look on the lighter side of things too. Don't you agree?

HORNE: Oh yes, Mr. King.

BARROW: Yes, Mr. King.

KING: Also gives a sense of belonging. Work together and play together. Office work can become so impersonal. We like to foster . . . to foster something . . . very different. You know what I mean?

HORNE: Oh yes, Mr. King.

BARROW: Yes, Mr. King.

KING: You interested in sailing, by any chance? You're quite welcome to come down to my boat at Poole any weekend— do a bit of sailing along the coast.

HORNE: Oh, thank you, Mr. King.

BARROW: Thank you, Mr. King.

JOYCE *and* EILEEN, *whispering.*

JOYCE [*slyly*]: Eh, what about going over and cheering up old Albert?

EILEEN: What for?

JOYCE: Well, he looks a bit gloomy, don't he?

EILEEN: I don't want to go over. You go over.

JOYCE: No, come on. You come over.

EILEEN: What for?

JOYCE: Cheer him up. For a bit of fun.

EILEEN: Oh, you're awful.

JOYCE: Come on. Come over.

KING [*to* RYAN]: Can I fill your glass, Ryan?

[RYAN *nods, and smiles.*]

Can't leave you without a drink, can we? The guest of honour.

JOYCE *and* EILEEN *sit either side of* ALBERT *on a divan.*

JOYCE: Mind if we join you?

ALBERT: Oh, hullo.

EILEEN: Enjoying the party?

JOYCE: What are you sitting all gloomy about?

ALBERT: I'm not gloomy, I'm just sitting, drinking. Feel a bit tired, actually.

JOYCE: Why, what have you been doing?

ALBERT: Nothing.

JOYCE: You just said you were tired. Eh, move up, I'm on the edge.

ALBERT: Sorry.

EILEEN: Eh, mind out, you're squashing me.

ALBERT: Oh . . .

JOYCE: You squash her, she won't mind.

EILEEN [*laughing*]: Oh, Joyce!

GIDNEY, *with a smile, watching.*

JOYCE: Come on, tell us, what are you tired about?

ALBERT: Oh, just work, I suppose.

JOYCE: I've been working too. I'm not tired. I love work.
Don't you, Eileen? [*She leans across him to speak.*]

EILEEN: Oh yes, I love work.

ALBERT: No, I'm not tired, really. I'm all right.

EILEEN: He looks tired.

JOYCE: You've been living it up. Women.

EILEEN: I'll bet.

JOYCE: Females.

*The girls giggle.*

ALBERT [*with an uncertain smile*]: No, I wouldn't . . .

EILEEN: Eh, mind your drink. My best taffeta.

JOYCE: He's not bad looking when you get close.

EILEEN: Quite nice when you get close.

ALBERT: Thanks for the compliment.

EILEEN: You got a flat of your own?

ALBERT: No. Have you?

EILEEN [*forlornly*]: No.

JOYCE: You live with your mother, don't you?

ALBERT: Yes.

JOYCE: Does she look after you all right, then?

ALBERT: Yes, she . . . [*He stands.*] I'm just going to the bar.

JOYCE: So are we.

EILEEN: Me too.

*They follow.*

KING: Well, now everyone . . .

JOYCE: I'm having gin.

ALBERT: Gin? Wait a minute . . .

KING: Just a minute, everyone, can I have your attention?

GIDNEY [*to* JOYCE]: Didn't make much impression, did you?

JOYCE: Didn't I?

KING: Just for a moment, please . . .

GIDNEY: Eh, Stokes, pay attention, will you?

ALBERT: What?

GIDNEY: Mr. King wants your attention.

KING: I'd just like to propose a toast to our guest of honour, Mr. Ryan. Gidney!

GIDNEY: Yes?

ALBERT: Here's your gin, then.

JOYCE: Thanks.

KING [*to* GIDNEY]: Go and get Kedge out of that corner, will you? Now, as you know, we're all gathered here tonight to pay our respects to our old friend and colleague, Mr. Ryan . . .

KEDGE *and* BETTY *are locked together in the armchair.* GIDNEY *taps* KEDGE *on the shoulder.*

GIDNEY: Mr. King wants to know if you'll honour the party with your presence.

KEDGE [*jumping up*]: Oh, sorry. [BETTY, *thrown off, falls. He picks her up.*] Sorry.

KING: We've all known Mr. Ryan for a very long time. Of course, I've known him myself much longer than anyone here—

KEDGE: For he's a jolly good fellow—

KING: Wait! Very glad for your enthusiasm, Mr. Kedge. Your heart, I am quite sure, is in the right place.

*General laughter.*

ALBERT, EILEEN, JOYCE, SEELEY *and* GIDNEY *stand in a group around* MR. RYAN'S *chair.*

But please allow me to toast Mr. Ryan first and then the floor is yours. Well, as I was saying, the whole department is here tonight to pay tribute to a man who from time immemorial has become, how shall I put it, the very core of our little community. I remember Mr. Ryan sitting at his very own desk the first time my father brought me into the office—

*A sharp scream and stiffening from* EILEEN. *All turn to her.*

Good heavens!

GIDNEY: What is it?

AD LIB: What's happened? Eileen, what's the matter?

EILEEN: Someone touched me!

JOYCE: Touched you?

EILEEN: Someone touched me! Someone—!

BETTY: What did he do?

KEDGE: Touched you? What did he do?

JOYCE: What did he do, Eileen?

EILEEN: He . . . he . . . he took a liberty!

KEDGE: Go on! Who did?

EILEEN *turns and stares at* ALBERT. *Silence. All stare at* ALBERT.

ALBERT: What are you looking at me for?

GIDNEY [*muttering*]: Good God . . .

*Tense, embarrassed pause.*

HORNE [*at the door, whispering*]: What did he do, touch her?

BARROW [*open-mouthed*]: Yes.

HORNE [*wide-eyed*]: Where?

*They look at each other, open-mouthed and wide-eyed.*

ALBERT: What are you looking at me for?

KING: Please, now . . . can we possibly . . . I mean . . .

EILEEN [*in a voice of reproach, indignation and horror*]: Albert!

ALBERT: What do you mean?

SEELEY: How does she know it was Albert?

KEDGE: Wonder what he did. Made her jump didn't he?

ALBERT: Now look, wait a minute, this is absolutely ridiculous—

GIDNEY: Ridiculous, eh? I'll say it is. What do you think you're up to?

EILEEN: Yes, I was just standing there, suddenly this hand . . .

JOYCE: I could tell he was that sort.

*The camera closes on* MR. RYAN'S *hand, resting comfortably on his knee, and then to his face which, smiling vaguely, is inclined to the ceiling. It must be quite clear from the expression that it was his hand which strayed.*

GIDNEY: Come out here, Albert.

ALBERT: Don't pull me. What are you doing?

SEELEY: How do you know it was him?

ALBERT [*throwing off* GIDNEY'S *hand*]: Let go of me!

SEELEY: What are you pulling him for?

GIDNEY: You keep out of this.

KING [*nervously*]: Now please let me continue my toast, ladies and gentlemen. Really, you must settle this elsewhere.

SEELEY: We don't even know what he's supposed to have done.

ALBERT: I didn't do anything.

GIDNEY: We can guess what he did.

KING [*at speed*]: We are all collected here tonight in honour of Mr. Ryan and to present him with a token of our affection—

JOYCE [*to* ALBERT]: You snake!

SEELEY: Well, what did he do? What's he supposed to have done?

ALBERT: She doesn't know what she's talking about.

SEELEY: Come on, what's he supposed to have done, Eileen, anyway?

EILEEN: Mind your own business.

JOYCE: You don't think she's going to tell you, do you?

GIDNEY: Look, Seeley, why don't you shut up?

SEELEY: Now don't talk to me like that, Gidney.

ALBERT: Don't worry about him, Seeley.

KING: As I have been trying to say—

JOYCE: You come over here, Eileen, sit down. She's upset, aren't you?

EILEEN [to SEELEY]: So would you be!

KING: Miss Phipps, would you mind composing yourself?

EILEEN: Composing myself!

GIDNEY: Come outside a minute, Albert.

KING: As I have been trying to say—

KEDGE [brightly]: I'm listening, Mr. King!

KING: What?

KEDGE: I'm listening. I'm with you.

KING: Oh, thank you. Thank you, my boy.

ALBERT: I'm going, anyway.

> ALBERT goes into the hall, followed by GIDNEY and SEELEY. The door shuts behind them.

GIDNEY: Wait a minute, Stokes.

ALBERT: What do you want?

GIDNEY: I haven't been satisfied with your . . . sort of . . . behaviour for some time, you know that, don't you?

ALBERT: You haven't . . . you haven't what?

GIDNEY: For instance, there was that bloody awful game of football you played when you threw the game away last Saturday that I've got on my mind, besides one or two other things!

SEELEY: Eh look, Gidney, you're talking like a prize—

GIDNEY [viciously]: I've told you to keep out of this.

ALBERT [tensely]: I'm going, anyway.

GIDNEY: Wait a minute, let's have it out. What do you think you're up to?

ALBERT: Look, I've told you—

GIDNEY: What did you think you were doing with that girl?

ALBERT: I didn't touch her.

GIDNEY: I'm responsible for that girl. She's a good friend of mine. I know her uncle.

ALBERT: Do you?

SEELEY: You know, you're being so stupid, Gidney—

GIDNEY: Seeley, I can take you any day, you know that, don't you?

SEELEY: Go on!

GIDNEY: Any day.

SEELEY: You can take me any day?

GIDNEY: Any day.

SEELEY: Well, go on, then. Go on . . . if you can take me . . .

ALBERT: Seeley—

SEELEY: No, if he says he can take me, if he can take me any day . . .

*The door opens slightly.* HORNE *and* BARROW *peer out.*

ALBERT: Gidney, why don't you . . . why don't you get back to the party?

GIDNEY: I was telling you, Albert—

ALBERT: Stokes.

GIDNEY: I was telling you, Albert, that if you're going to behave like a boy of ten in mixed company—

ALBERT: I told you my name's Stokes!

GIDNEY: Don't be childish, Albert.

*A sudden silence.* MR. KING'S *voice from the room.*

KING: . . . and for his unfailing good humour and cheeriness, Mr. Ryan will always be remembered at Hislop, King and Martindale!

*Scattered applause.* HORNE, *caught by their stares, shuts the door hastily.*

ALBERT [*going to the door.*]: Goodnight.

GIDNEY [*obstructing him*]: Go back and apologize.

ALBERT: What for?

GIDNEY: For insulting a lady. Mate. A lady. Something to do with breeding. But I suppose you're too bloody backward to know anything about that.

ALBERT: You're talking right out of your hat.

SEELEY: Right out of the bowler.

GIDNEY [*to* SEELEY]: No one invited you out here, did they?

SEELEY: Who invited you?

GIDNEY: I'm talking to this man on behalf of the firm! Unless I get a satisfactory explanation I shall think seriously about recommending his dismissal.

ALBERT: Get out of my way, will you?

GIDNEY: Acting like an animal all over the place—

ALBERT: Move out of it!

GIDNEY [*breathlessly*]: I know your trouble.

ALBERT: Oh, yes?

GIDNEY: Yes, sticks out a mile.

ALBERT: Does it?

GIDNEY: Yes.

ALBERT: What's my trouble then?

GIDNEY [*very deliberately*]: You're a mother's boy. That's what you are. That's your trouble. You're a mother's boy.

ALBERT *hits him. There is a scuffle.* SEELEY *tries to part them. The three rock back and forth in the hall: confused blows, words and grunts.*

*The door of the room opens. Faces.* MR. KING *comes out.*

KING: What in heaven's name is going on here!

*The scuffle stops. A short silence.* ALBERT *opens the front door, goes out and slams it behind him. He stands on the doorstep, breathing heavily, his face set.*

## SCENE TWO

*The kitchen.*

MRS. STOKES *is asleep, her head resting on the table, the cards disordered. The clock ticks. It is twelve o'clock. The front door opens slowly.* ALBERT *comes in, closes the door softly, stops, looks across to the open kitchen door, sees his mother, and begins to creep up the stairs with great stealth. The camera follows him. Her voice stops him.*

MOTHER: Albert!

*He stops.*

Albert! Is that you?

*She goes to the kitchen door.*

What are you creeping up the stairs for? Might have been a burglar. What would I have done then?

*He descends slowly.*

Creeping up the stairs like that. Give anyone a fright. Creeping up the stairs like that. You leave me in the house all alone . . . [*She stops and regards him.*] Look at you! Look at your suit. What's the matter with your tie, it's all crumpled, I pressed it for you this morning. Well, I won't even ask any questions. That's all. You look a disgrace.

*He walks past her into the kitchen, goes to the sink and pours himself a glass of water. She follows him.*

What have you been doing, mucking about with girls?

*She begins to pile the cards.*

Mucking about with girls, I suppose. Do you know what the time is? I fell asleep, right here at this table, waiting for you. I don't know what your father would say. Coming in this time of night. It's after twelve o'clock. In a state like that. Drunk, I suppose. I suppose your dinner's ruined. Well, if you want to make a convenience out of your own home, that's your business. I'm only your mother, I don't suppose that counts for much these days. I'm not saying any more. If you want to go mucking about with girls, that's your business.

*She takes his dinner out of the oven.*

Well, anyway, you'll have your dinner. You haven't eaten a single thing all night.

*She places a plate on the table and gets knife and fork. He stands by the sink, sipping water.*

I wouldn't mind if you found a really nice girl and brought her home and introduced her to your mother, brought her home for dinner, I'd know you were sincere, if she was a really nice girl, she'd be like a daughter to me. But you've never brought a girl home here in your life. I suppose you're ashamed of your mother.
[*Pause.*]
Come on, it's all dried up. I kept it on a low light. I couldn't even go up to Grandma's room and have a look round because there wasn't any bulb, you might as well eat it.

*He stands.*

What's the matter, are you drunk? Where did you go, to one of those pubs in the West End? You'll get into serious trouble, my boy, if you frequent those places, I'm warning you. Don't you read the papers?
[*Pause.*]
I hope you're satisfied, anyway. The house in darkness, I wasn't going to break my neck going down to that cellar

to look for a bulb, you come home looking like I don't know what, anyone would think you gave me a fortune out of your wages. Yes. I don't say anything, do I? I keep quiet about what you expect me to manage on. I never grumble. I keep a lovely home, I bet there's none of the boys in your firm better fed than you are. I'm not asking for gratitude. But one things hurts me, Albert, and I'll tell you what it is. Not for years, not for years, have you come up to me and said, Mum, I love you, like you did when you were a little boy. You've never said it without me having to ask you. Not since before your father died. And he was a good man. He had high hopes of you. I've never told you, Albert, about the high hopes he had of you. I don't know what you do with all your money. But don't forget what it cost us to rear you, my boy, I've never told you about the sacrifices we made, you wouldn't care, anyway. Telling me lies about going to the firm's party. They've got a bit of respect at that firm, that's why we sent you there, to start off your career, they wouldn't let you carry on like that at one of their functions. Mr. King would have his eye on you. I don't know where you've been. Well, if you don't want to lead a clean life it's your lookout, if you want to go mucking about with all sorts of bits of girls, if you're content to leave your own mother sitting here till midnight, and I wasn't feeling well, anyway, I didn't tell you because I didn't want to upset you, I keep things from you, you're the only one I've got, but what do you care, you don't care, you don't care, the least you can do is sit down and eat the dinner I cooked for you, specially for you, it's Shepherd's Pie—

ALBERT *lunges to the table, picks up the clock and violently raises it above his head. A stifled scream from the* MOTHER.

# Act Three

*The coffee stall, shuttered.*

ALBERT *is leaning against it. He is sweating. He is holding the butt of a cigarette. There is a sound of a foot on gravel. He starts, the butt burns his hand, he drops it and turns. A* GIRL *is looking at him. She smiles.*

GIRL: Good evening.
  [*Pause.*]
  What are you doing?
  [*Pause.*]
  What are you doing out at this time of night?

  *She moves closer to him.*

  I live just round the corner.

  *He stares at her.*

  Like to? Chilly out here, isn't it? Come on.
  [*Pause.*]
  Come on.

  *He goes with her.*


## SCENE TWO

*The* GIRL'S *room. The door opens. She comes in. Her manner has changed from the seductive. She is brisk and nervous.*

GIRL: Come in. Don't slam the door. Shut it gently. I'll light the fire. Chilly out, don't you find? Have you got a match?

*He walks across the room.*

Please don't walk so heavily. Please. There's no need to
let . . . to let the whole house know you're here. Life's
difficult enough as it is. Have you got a match?
ALBERT: No, I . . . I don't think I have.
GIRL: Oh, God, you'd think you'd have a match.

*He walks about.*

I say, would you mind taking your shoes off? You're
really making a dreadful row. Really, I can't bear . . .
noisy . . . people.

*He looks at his shoes, begins to untie one. The* GIRL *searches
for matches on the mantelpiece, upon which are a number of
articles and objects, including a large alarm clock.*

I know I had one somewhere.
ALBERT: I've got a lighter.
GIRL: You can't light a gasfire with a lighter. You'd burn your
fingers.

*She bends down to the hearth.*

Where are the damn things? This is ridiculous. I die
without the fire. I simply die. [*She finds the box.*] Ah, here
we are. At last.

*She turns on the gas fire and lights it. He watches her. She
puts the matchbox on the mantelpiece and picks up a photo.*

Do you like this photo? It's of my little girl. She's staying
with friends. Rather fine, isn't she? Very aristocratic
features, don't you think? She's at a very select boarding
school at the moment, actually. In . . . Hereford, very
near Hereford. [*She puts the photo back.*] I shall be going
down for the prize day shortly. You do look idiotic standing
there with one shoe on and one shoe off. All lop-sided.

ALBERT *pulls at the lace of his other shoe.  The lace breaks.
He swears shortly under his breath.*

GIRL [*sharply*]: Do you mind not saying words like that?
ALBERT: I didn't . . .
GIRL: I heard you curse.
ALBERT: My lace broke.
GIRL: That's no excuse.
ALBERT: What did I say?
GIRL: I'm sorry, I can't bear that sort of thing. It's just . . .
not in my personality.
ALBERT: I'm sorry.
GIRL: It's quite all right. It's just . . . something in my
nature. I've got to think of my daughter, too, you know.

*She crouches by the fire.*

Come near the fire a minute. Sit down.

*He goes towards a small stool.*

Not on that! That's my seat. It's my own stool. I did the
needlework myself. A long time ago.

*He sits in a chair, opposite.*

Which do you prefer, electric or gas? For a fire, I mean?
ALBERT [*holding his forehead, muttering*]: I don't know.
GIRL: There's no need to be rude, it was a civil question. I
prefer gas. Or a log fire, of course. They have them in
Switzerland.
[*Pause.*]
Have you got a headache?
ALBERT: No.
GIRL: I didn't realize you had a lighter. You don't happen to
have any cigarettes on you, I suppose?
ALBERT: No.
GIRL: I'm very fond of a smoke. After dinner. With a glass of
wine. Or before dinner, with sherry.

*She stands and taps the mantelpiece, her eyes roaming over it.*

You look as if you've had a night out. Where have you been? Had a nice time?

ALBERT: Quite . . . quite nice.

GIRL [*sitting on the stool*]: What do you do?

ALBERT: I . . . work in films.

GIRL: Films? Really? What do you do?

ALBERT: I'm an assistant director.

GIRL: Really? How funny. I used to be a continuity girl. But I gave it up.

ALBERT [*tonelessly*]: What a pity.

GIRL: Yes, I'm beginning to think you're right. You meet such a good class of people. Of course, now you say you're an assistant director I can see what you mean. I mean, I could tell you had breeding the moment I saw you. You looked a bit washed out, perhaps, but there was no mistaking the fact that you had breeding. I'm extremely particular, you see. I do like a certain amount of delicacy in men . . . a certain amount . . . a certain degree . . . a certain amount of refinement. You do see my point? Some men I couldn't possibly entertain. Not even if I was . . . starving. I don't want to be personal, but that word you used, when you broke your lace, it made me shiver, I'm just not that type, made me wonder if you were as well bred as I thought . . .

*He wipes his face with his hand.*

You do look hot. Why are you so hot? It's chilly. Yes, you remind me . . . I saw the most ghastly horrible fight before, there was a man, one man, he was sweating . . . sweating. You haven't been in a fight, by any chance? I don't know how men can be so bestial. It's hardly much fun for women, I can tell you. I don't want someone else's blood on my carpet.

ALBERT *chuckles*.

What are you laughing at?
ALBERT: Nothing.
GIRL: It's not in the least funny.

ALBERT *looks up at the mantelpiece. His gaze rests there.*

What are you looking at?
ALBERT [*ruminatively*]: That's a nice big clock.

*It is twenty past two.*

GIRL [*with fatigue*]: Yes, it's late, I suppose we might as well
. . . Haven't you got a cigarette?
ALBERT: No.
GIRL [*jumping up*]: I'm sure I have, somewhere. [*She goes to
the table.*] Yes, here we are, I knew I had. I have to hide
them. The woman who comes in to do my room, she's very
light-fingered. I don't know why she comes in at all. Nobody wants her, all she does is spy on me, but I'm obliged
to put up with her, this room is serviced. Which means
I have to pay a pretty penny.

*She lights her cigarette.*

It's a dreadful area, too. I'm thinking of moving. The
neighbourhood is full of people of no class at all. I just don't
fit in.
ALBERT: Is that clock right?
GIRL: People have told me, the most distinguished people,
that I could go anywhere. You could go anywhere, they've
told me, you could be anything. I'm quite well educated,
you know. My father was a . . . he was a military man.
In the Army. Actually it was a relief to speak to you. I
haven't . . . spoken to anyone for some hours.

ALBERT *suddenly coughs violently.*

Oh, please don't do that! Use your handkerchief!

*He sighs, and groans.*

What on earth's the matter with you? What have you been doing tonight?

*He looks at her and smiles.*

ALBERT: Nothing.
GIRL: Really?

*She belches.*

Oh, excuse me. I haven't eaten all day. I had a tooth out. Hiccoughs come from not eating, don't they? Do you . . . do you want one of these?

*She throws him a cigarette, which he slowly lights.*

I mean, I'm no different from any other girl. In fact, I'm better. These so-called respectable girls, for instance, I'm sure they're much worse than I am. Well, you're an assistant director—all your continuity girls and secretaries, I'll bet they're . . . very loose.
ALBERT: Uh.
GIRL: Do you know what I've actually heard? I've heard that respectable married women, solicitors' wives, go out and pick men up when their husbands are out on business! Isn't that fantastic? I mean, they're supposed to be . . . they're supposed to be respectable!
ALBERT [*muttering*]: Fantastic.
GIRL: I beg your pardon?
ALBERT: I said it was fantastic.
GIRL: It is. You're right. Quite fantastic. Here's one thing, though. There's one thing that's always fascinated me. How far do men's girl friends go? I've often wondered.
[*Pause.*]
Eh?
ALBERT: Depends.

GIRL: Yes, I suppose it must.

   [*Pause.*]

   You mean on the girl?

ALBERT: What?

GIRL: You mean it depends on the girl?

ALBERT: It would do, yes.

GIRL: Quite possibly. I must admit that with your continuity girls and secretaries, I don't see why you . . . had to approach me. . . . Have you been on the town tonight, then? With a continuity girl?

ALBERT: You're a bit . . . worried about continuity girls, aren't you?

GIRL: Only because I've been one myself. I know what they're like. No better than they should be.

ALBERT: When were you a . . .?

GIRL: Years ago! [*Standing.*] You're nosey, aren't you?

*She goes to the window.*

Sometimes I wish the night would never end. I like sleeping. I could sleep . . . on and on.

ALBERT *stands and picks up the clock.*

Yes, you can see the station from here. All the trains go out, right through the night.

*He stares at the clock.*

I suppose we might as well . . . [*She turns and sees him.*] What are you doing? [*She crosses to him.*] What are you doing with that clock?

*He looks at her, slowly.*

Mmnn?

ALBERT: Admiring it.

GIRL: It's a perfectly ordinary clock. Give me it. I've seen too many people slip things into their pockets before now, as soon as your back's turned. Nothing personal, of course. [*She puts it back.*] Mind your ash! Don't spill it all over the floor! I have to keep this carpet immaculate. Otherwise the charlady, she's always looking for excuses for telling tales. Here. Here's an ashtray. Use it, please.

*She gives it to him. He stares at her.*

Sit down. Sit down. Don't stand about like that. What are you staring at me for?

*He sits. She studies him.*

Where's your wife?
ALBERT: Nowhere.

*She stubs her cigarette.*

GIRL: And what film are you making at the moment?
ALBERT: I'm on holiday.
GIRL: Where do you work?
ALBERT: I'm a free lance.
GIRL: You're . . . rather young to be in such a . . . high position, aren't you?
ALBERT: Oh?
GIRL [*laughs*]: You amuse me. You interest me. I'm a bit of a psychologist, you know. You're very young to be—what you said you were. There's something childish in your face, almost retarded. [*She laughs.*] I do like that word. I'm not being personal, of course . . . just being . . . psychological. Of course, I can see you're one for the girls. Don't know why you had to pick on me, at this time of night, really rather forward of you. I'm a respectable mother, you know, with a child at boarding school. You couldn't call me . . . anything else. All I do, I just entertain a few gentlemen, of my own choice, now and again. What girl doesn't?

*His hand screws the cigarette. He lets it fall on the carpet.*

[*Outraged.*] What do you think you're doing?

*She stares at him.*

Pick it up! Pick that up, I tell you! It's my carpet!

*She lunges towards it.*

It's not my carpet, they'll make me pay—

*His hand closes upon hers as she reaches for it.*

What are you doing? Let go. Treating my place like a pigsty. [*She looks up at him as he bends over her.*] Let me go. You're burning my carpet!

ALBERT [*quietly, intensely*]: Sit down.

GIRL: How dare you?

ALBERT: Shut up. Sit down.

GIRL [*struggling*]: What are you doing?

ALBERT [*erratically, trembling, but with quiet command*]: Don't scream. I'm warning you.

*He lifts her by her wrist and presses her down on to the stool.*

No screaming. I warn you.

GIRL: What's the—?

ALBERT [*through his teeth*]: Be quiet. I told you to be quiet. Now you be quiet.

GIRL: What are you going to do?

ALBERT [*seizing the clock from the mantelpiece*]: DON'T MUCK ME ABOUT!

*She freezes with terror.*

See this? One crack with this . . . just one crack . . . [*Viciously.*] Who do you think you are? You talk too much, you know that. You never stop talking. Just because you're a woman you think you can get away with it. [*Bending over her.*] You've made a mistake, this time. You've picked the wrong man.

*He begins to grow in stature and excitement, passing the clock from hand to hand.*

You're all the same, you see, you're all the same, you're just a dead weight round my neck. What makes you think . . . [*He begins to move about the room, at one point half crouching, at another standing upright, as if exercising his body.*] . . . What makes you think you can . . . tell me . . . yes . . . It's the same as this business about the light in Grandma's room. Always something. Always something. [*To her.*] My ash? I'll put it where I like! You see this clock? Watch your step. Just watch your step.

GIRL: Stop this. What are you—?

ALBERT [*seizing her wrist, with trembling, controlled violence*]: Watch your step! [*Stammering.*] I've had—I've had—I've had—just about enough. Get it? . . . You know what I did?

*He looks at her and chuckles.*

Don't be so frightened.

GIRL: I . . .

ALBERT [*casually*]: Don't be so frightened.

*He squats by her, still holding the clock.*

I'm just telling you. I'm just telling you, that's all. [*Breathlessly.*] You haven't got any breeding. She hadn't either. And what about those girls tonight? Same kind. And that one. I didn't touch her!

GIRL [*almost inaudible*]: What you been doing?

ALBERT: I've got as many qualifications as the next man. Let's get that quite . . . straight. And I got the answer to her. I got the answer to her, you see, tonight. . . . I finished the conversation . . . I finished it . . . I finished her . . .

*She squirms. He raises the clock.*

With this clock! [*Trembling.*] One . . . crack . . . with

. . . this. . . clock . . . finished! [*Thoughtfully.*] Of course, I loved her, really. [*He suddenly sees the photograph on the mantelpiece, puts the clock down and takes it. The* GIRL *half rises and gasps, watching him. He looks at the photo curiously.*] Uhhh ? . . . Your daughter ? . . . This a photo of your daughter ? . . . Uuuh? [*He breaks the frame and takes out the photo.*]

GIRL [*rushes at him*]. Leave that!

ALBERT [*dropping the frame and holding the photo*]: Is it?

*The* GIRL *grabs at it.* ALBERT *clutches her wrist. He holds her at arm's length.*

GIRL: Leave that! [*Writhing.*] What? Don't—it's mine!

ALBERT [*turns the photo over and reads back*]: 'Class Three Classical, Third Prize, Bronze Medal, Twickenham Competition, nineteen thirty-three.' [*He stares at her. The* GIRL *stands, shivering and whimpering.*] You liar. That's you.

GIRL: It's not!

ALBERT: That's not your daughter. It's you! You're just a fake, you're just all lies!

GIRL: Scum! Filthy scum!

ALBERT, *twisting her wrist, moves suddenly to her. The* GIRL *cringing, falls back into her chair.*

ALBERT [*warningly*]: Mind how you talk to me. [*He crumples the photo.*]

GIRL [*moans*]: My daughter. My little girl. My little baby girl.

ALBERT: Get up.

GIRL: No . . .

ALBERT: Get up! Up!

*She stands.*

Walk over there, to the wall. Go on! Get over there. Do as you're told. Do as I'm telling you. I'm giving the orders here.

*She walks to the wall.*

Stop!
GIRL [*whimpering*]: What . . . do you want me to do?
ALBERT: Just keep your big mouth closed, for a start.

*He frowns uncertainly.*

Cover your face!

*She does so. He looks about, blinking.*

Yes. That's right. [*He sees his shoes.*] Come on, come on,
pick up those shoes. Those shoes! Pick them up!

*She looks for the shoes and picks them up.*

That's right. [*He sits.*] Bring them over here. Come on.
That's right. Put them on.

*He extends his foot.*

GIRL: You're . . .
ALBERT: On! Right on. That's it. That's it. That's more like
it. That's . . . more like it! Good. Lace them! Good.

*He stands. She crouches.*

*Silence.*

*He shivers and murmurs with the cold. He looks about the room.*

ALBERT: It's cold.
[*Pause.*]
Ooh, it's freezing.
GIRL [*whispering*]: The fire's gone.
ALBERT [*looking at the window*]: What's that? Looks like light.
Ooh, it's perishing. [*Looks about, muttering.*] What a dump.
Not staying here. Getting out of this place.

*He shivers and drops the clock. He looks down at it. She too.*
*He kicks it across the room.*

[*With a smile, softly.*] So you . . . bear that in mind. Mind how you talk to me.

*He goes to door, then turns.*

[*Flipping half a crown to her.*] Buy yourself a seat . . . buy yourself a seat at a circus.

*He opens the door and goes.*

## SCENE THREE

*The house.*
*The front door opens.* ALBERT *comes in, a slight smile on his face. He saunters across the hall into the kitchen, takes off his jacket and throws it across the room. The same with his tie. He sits heavily, loosely, in a chair, his legs stretched out. Stretching his arms, he yawns luxuriously, scratches his head with both hands and stares ruminatively at the ceiling, a smile on his face. His mother's voice calls his name.*

MOTHER [*from the stairs*]: Albert!

*His body freezes. His gaze comes down. His legs slowly come together. He looks in front of him.*
*His* MOTHER *comes into the room, in her dressing gown. She stands, looking at him.*

Do you know what the time is?
[*Pause.*]
Where have you been?
[*Pause.*]
[*Reproachfully, near to tears.*] I don't know what to say to you, Albert. To raise your hand to your own mother. You've never done that before in your life. To threaten your own mother.
[*Pause.*]

That clock would have hurt me, Albert. And you'd have been . . . I know you'd have been very sorry. Aren't I a good mother to you? Everything I do is . . . is for your own good. You should know that. You're all I've got.

*She looks at his slumped figure. Her reproach turns to solicitude.*

[*Gently.*] Look at you. You look washed out. Oh, you look . . . I don't understand what could have come over you.

*She takes a chair and sits close to him.*

Listen, Albert, I'll tell you what I'm going to do. I'm going to forget it. You see? I'm going to forget all about it. We'll have your holiday in a fortnight. We can go away.

*She strokes his hand.*

We'll go away . . . together.
[*Pause.*]
It's not as if you're a bad boy . . . you're a good boy . . . I know you are . . . it's not as if you're really bad, Albert, you're not . . . you're not bad, you're good . . . you're not a bad boy, Albert, I know you're not . . .
[*Pause.*]
You're good, you're not bad, you're a good boy . . . I know you are . . . you are, aren't you?

# NIGHT SCHOOL

*Night School* was first presented by Associated Rediffusion Television on 21 July 1960, with the following cast:

| | |
|---|---|
| ANNIE | Iris Vandeleur |
| WALTER | Milo O'Shea |
| MILLY | Jane Eccles |
| SALLY | Vivien Merchant |
| SOLTO | Martin Miller |
| TULLY | Bernard Spear |

Directed by Joan Kemp-Welch


It was later performed on the B.B.C. Third Programme on 25 September 1966 in the version printed here, with the following cast:

| | |
|---|---|
| ANNIE | Mary O'Farrell |
| WALTER | John Hollis |
| MILLY | Sylvia Coleridge |
| SALLY | Prunella Scales |
| SOLTO | Sydney Tafler |
| TULLY | Preston Lockwood |
| BARBARA | Barbara Mitchell |
| MAVIS | Carol Marsh |

Directed by Guy Vaesen

*Living-room.*

ANNIE: Look at your raincoat. It's on the floor.

WALTER: I'll hang it up. I'll take the case upstairs, eh?

ANNIE: Have your tea. Go on, have your tea. Don't worry about taking the case upstairs.

*Pause.*

WALTER: Lovely cake.

ANNIE: Do you like it? I've had to lay off cake. They was giving me heartburn. Go on, have another piece.

WALTER: Ah well, the place looks marvellous.

ANNIE: I gave it a nice clean-out before you came.

*Pause.*

Well, Wally, how did they treat you this time, eh?

WALTER: Marvellous.

ANNIE: I didn't expect you back so soon. I thought you was staying longer this time.

WALTER: No, I wasn't staying longer.

ANNIE: Milly's not been well.

WALTER: Oh? What's the matter with her?

ANNIE: She'll be down in a minute, she heard you come.

WALTER: I brought some chocolates for her.

ANNIE: I can't stand chocolates.

WALTER: I know that. That's why I didn't bring any for you.

ANNIE: You remembered, eh?

WALTER: Oh, yes.

ANNIE: Yes, she's been having a rest upstairs. All I do, I run up and down them stairs all day long. What about the other day? I was up doing those curtains, I came over terrible. Then she says I shouldn't have done them that way. I should have done them the other way.

WALTER: What's the matter with the curtains?

ANNIE: She says they're not hanging properly. She says I should have done them the other way. She likes them the other way. She lies up there upstairs. I'm older than she is.

ANNIE *pours herself and* WALTER *more tea.*

I went out and got that cake the minute we got your letter.

WALTER [*sighing*]: Ah, you know, I've been thinking for months . . . you know that? . . . months . . . I'll come back here . . . I'll lie on my bed . . . I'll see the curtains blowing by the window . . . I'll have a good rest, eh?

ANNIE: There she is, she's moving herself. You got a bit of the sun.

WALTER: I'm going to take it easy for a few weeks.

ANNIE: You should. It's silly. You should have a rest for a few weeks.

*Pause.*

WALTER: How's Mr. Solto?

ANNIE: He's still the best landlord in the district. You wouldn't get a better landlord in any district.

WALTER: You're good tenants to him.

ANNIE: He's so kind. He's almost one of the family. Except he doesn't live here. As a matter of fact, he hasn't been to tea for months.

WALTER: I'm going to ask him to lend me some money.

ANNIE: She's coming down.

WALTER: What's a couple of hundred to him? Nothing.

ANNIE [*whispering*]: Don't say a word about the curtains.

WALTER: Eh?

ANNIE: Don't mention about the curtains. About the hanging. About what I told you about what she said about the way I hung the curtains. Don't say a word. Here she comes.

MILLY *enters.*

WALTER [*kissing her*]: Aunty Milly.

MILLY: Did she give you a bit of cake?

WALTER: Marvellous cake.

MILLY: I told her to go and get it.

WALTER: I haven't had a bit of cake like that for nine solid months.

MILLY: It comes from down the road.

WALTER: Here you are, Aunty, here's some chocolates.

MILLY: He didn't forget that I like chocolates.

ANNIE: He didn't forget that I don't like chocolates.

MILLY: Nutty? Are they nutty?

WALTER: I picked them specially for the nuts. They were the nuttiest ones they had there.

ANNIE: Sit down, Milly. Don't stand up.

MILLY: I've been sitting down, I've been lying down. I got to stand up now and again.

WALTER: You haven't been so well, eh?

MILLY: Middling. Only middling.

ANNIE: I'm only middling as well.

MILLY: Yes, Annie's only been middling.

WALTER: Well, I'm back now, eh?

MILLY: How did they treat you this time?

WALTER: Very well. Very well.

MILLY: When you going back?

WALTER: I'm not going back.

MILLY: You ought to be ashamed of yourself, Walter, spending half your life in prison. Where do you think that's going to get you?

WALTER: Half my life? What do you mean? Twice, that's all.

ANNIE: What about Borstal?

WALTER: That doesn't count.

MILLY: I wouldn't mind if you ever had a bit of luck, but what happens? Every time you move yourself they take you inside.

WALTER: I've finished with all that, anyway.

MILLY: Listen, I've told you before, if you're not clever in that way you should try something else, you should open up a little business—you could get the capital from Solto, he'll lend you some money. I mean, every time you put a foot outside the door they pick you up, they put you inside. What's the good of it?

ANNIE: You going to have a jam tart, Wally?

WALTER: Sure.

MILLY [*eats*]: Where'd you get the jam tarts?

ANNIE: Round the corner.

MILLY: Round the corner? I thought I told you to get them down the road.

ANNIE: He didn't have any down the road.

MILLY: Why, he'd run out?

ANNIE: I don't know if he'd made any today.

MILLY: What are they like?

WALTER: Lovely. [*He takes another. Eats. Pause.*]

MILLY: I've had to lay off tarts, haven't I, Annie?

ANNIE: They was giving her heartburn.

MILLY: I had to lay off. I had to lay right off tarts, since just after Easter.

ANNIE: I bet you never had a tart in prison, Wally.

WALTER: No, I couldn't lay my hands on one.

*Pause.*

MILLY: Well? Have you told him?

ANNIE: Told him what?

MILLY: You haven't told him?

WALTER: Told me what?

MILLY: Eh?

ANNIE: No, I haven't.

MILLY: Why not?

ANNIE: I wasn't going to tell him.

WALTER: Tell me what?

MILLY: You said you was going to tell him.

ANNIE: I didn't have the pluck.
WALTER: What's going on here? What's all this?

*Pause.*

ANNIE: Have a rock cake, Wally.
WALTER: No, thanks. I'm full up.
ANNIE: Go on, have a rock cake.
WALTER: No, I've had enough. Honest.
MILLY: Have a rock cake, come on.
WALTER: I can't, I'm full up!
ANNIE: I'll go and fill the pot.
MILLY: I'll go.
ANNIE: You can't go, come on, give me the pot. You can't go, you're not well.
MILLY: I'll go, come on, give me the pot.
ANNIE: I made the tea, why shouldn't I fill the pot?
MILLY: Can't I fill the pot for my own nephew!
WALTER: Now listen, what have you got to tell me—what's the matter? I come home from prison, I been away nine months, I come home for a bit of peace and quiet to recuperate. What's going on here?
MILLY: Well . . . we've let your room.
WALTER: You've what?
ANNIE: We've let your room.

*Pause.*

MILLY: Look, Wally, don't start making faces. How could we help ourselves?

*Pause.*

WALTER: You've done what?
ANNIE: We missed you.
MILLY: It gave us a bit of company.
ANNIE: Of course it did . . .

MILLY: It gave us a helping hand . . .

ANNIE: You spend half your time inside, we don't know when you're coming out . . .

MILLY: We only get the pension.

ANNIE: That's all we got, we only got the pension.

MILLY: She pays good money, she pays thirty-five and six a week . . .

ANNIE: She's down here every Friday morning with the rent.

MILLY: And she looks after her room, she's always dusting her room.

ANNIE: She helps me give a bit of a dust round the house.

MILLY: On the week-ends . . .

ANNIE: She leaves the bath as good as new . . .

MILLY: And you should see what she's done to her room.

ANNIE: Oh, you should see how she's made the room.

MILLY: She's made it beautiful, she's made it really pretty . . .

ANNIE: She's fitted up a bedside table lamp in there, hasn't she?

MILLY: She's always studying books . . .

ANNIE: She goes out to night school three nights a week.

MILLY: She's a young girl.

ANNIE: She's a very clean girl.

MILLY: She's quiet . . .

ANNIE: She's a homely girl . . .

*Pause.*

WALTER: What's her name?

ANNIE: Sally . . .

WALTER: Sally what?

MILLY: Sally Gibbs.

WALTER: How long has she been here?

MILLY: She's been here about—when did she come?

ANNIE: She came about . . .

MILLY: Four months about . . . she's been here . . .

WALTER: What does she do, for a living?

MILLY: She teaches at a school.

WALTER: A school teacher!

MILLY: Yes.

WALTER: A school teacher! In my room.

*Pause.*

ANNIE: Wally, you'll like her.

WALTER: She's sleeping in my room!

MILLY: What's the matter with the put-u-up? You can have the put-u-up in here.

WALTER: The put-u-up? She's sleeping in my bed.

ANNIE: She's bought a lovely coverlet, she's put it on.

WALTER: A coverlet? I could go out now, I could pick up a coverlet as good as hers. What are you talking about coverlets for?

MILLY: Walter, don't shout at your aunt, she's deaf.

WALTER: I can't believe it. I come home after nine months in a dungeon.

ANNIE: The money's been a great help.

WALTER: Have I ever left you short of money?

MILLY: Yes!

WALTER: Well . . . not through my own fault. I've always done my best.

MILLY: And where's it got you?

WALTER: What's this, you reproaching me?

ANNIE: Your aunt's not one to go around reproaching people, Walter.

MILLY: Live and let live, that's my motto.

ANNIE: And mine.

MILLY: It's always been my motto, you ask anyone.

WALTER: Listen, you don't understand. This is my home. I live here. I've lived in that room for years—

ANNIE: On and off.

WALTER: You're asking me to sleep on that put-u-up? The

only person who ever slept on that put-u-up was Aunty Gracy. That's why she went to America.

MILLY: She slept in it for five years with Uncle Alf, Grace did. They never had a word of complaint.

WALTER: Uncle Alf! Honest, this has knocked me for . . . for six. I can't believe it. But I'll tell you one thing about that bed she's sleeping in.

ANNIE: What's the matter with it?

WALTER: There's nothing the matter with it. It's mine, that's all—I bought it.

ANNIE: So he did, Milly.

MILLY: You? I thought I bought it.

ANNIE: That's right. You did. I remember.

WALTER: You bought it, you went out and chose it, but who gave you the money to buy it?

ANNIE: Yes, he's right. He did.

WALTER: I mean . . . what's happened to my damn things? What's happened to my case? The one I left here?

ANNIE: Well, she didn't mind us leaving your things in the cupboard, did she, Milly?

WALTER: Things? That's my life's work!

*Pause.*

She'll have to go, that's all.

MILLY: She's not going.

WALTER: Why not?

ANNIE: She's not going to go.

MILLY: I should say not. She's staying.

*Pause.*

WALTER [*with fatigue*]: Why can't she sleep on the put-u-up?

ANNIE: Put a lovely girl like that on the put-u-up? In the dining-room?

WALTER: She's lovely, is she?

MILLY: You should see the beauty cream on her dressing-table.

WALTER: My dressing-table.

MILLY: I like a girl who looks after herself.

ANNIE: She gives herself a good going over every night.

MILLY: She's never out of the bath. Morning and night. On the nights she goes to night school, she has one before she goes out; other nights she has it just before she goes to bed.

WALTER: Well, she couldn't have it after she's gone to bed, could she?

*Pause.*

Night school? What kind of night school?

MILLY: She's studying foreign languages there. She's learning to speak two more languages.

ANNIE: Yes, you can smell her up and down the house.

WALTER: Smell her?

ANNIE: Lovely perfumes she puts on.

MILLY: Yes, I'll say that, it's a pleasure to smell her.

WALTER: Is it?

ANNIE: There's nothing wrong with a bit of perfume.

MILLY: We're not narrow-minded over a bit of perfume.

ANNIE: She's up to date, that's all.

MILLY: Up to the latest fashion.

ANNIE: I was, when I was a girl.

MILLY: What about me?

ANNIE: So were you. But you weren't as up to date as I was.

MILLY: I was. I didn't have anything coming over me.

*Pause.*

WALTER: Does she know where I've been?

ANNIE: Oh, yes.

WALTER: You told her I've been in the nick?

ANNIE: Oh, we told her, yes.

WALTER: Did you tell her why?

MILLY: Oh, no. Oh no, we didn't tell her why.

ANNIE: Oh, no, we didn't discuss that . . . But I mean it didn't worry her, did it, Milly? I mean she was very interested. Oh, she was terribly interested.

WALTER [*slowly*]: She was, was she?

ANNIE: Yes.

WALTER *stands abruptly, slamming the table.*

WALTER: Where am I going to put my case?

ANNIE: You can put it in the hall.

WALTER: The hall? That means I'll have to keep running out to the hall whenever I want anything.

*Pause.*

I can't live in these conditions for long. I'm used to something better. I'm used to privacy. I could have her walking in here any time of the day or night. This is the living-room. I don't want to share my meals with a stranger.

ANNIE: She only has bed and breakfast. I take it up to her room.

WALTER: What does she have?

ANNIE: She has a nice piece of bacon with a poached egg, and she enjoys every minute of it.

WALTER: For thirty-five and six a week? They're charging three pounds ten everywhere up and down the country. She's doing you. She's got hot and cold running water, every comfort, breakfast in a first-class bed. She's taking you for a ride.

ANNIE: No, she's not.

*Pause.*

WALTER: I left something in my room. I'm going to get it.

*He goes out and up the stairs. The bathroom door opens and*

SALLY *comes out. She descends the stairs half-way down. They meet.*

SALLY: Mr. Street?
WALTER: Yes.
SALLY: I'm so pleased to meet you. I've heard so much about you.
WALTER: Oh yes.

*Pause.*

I . . . er . . .
SALLY: Your aunts are charming people.
WALTER: Mmmm.

*Pause.*

SALLY: Are you glad to be back?
WALTER: I've left something in my room. I've got to get it.
SALLY: Oh, well, we'll meet again. Bye-bye.

*She goes to her room. He follows.*
*The footsteps stop.*

WALTER: Could I just . . .?
SALLY: What?
WALTER: Come in.
SALLY: Come in? But . . . well, yes . . . do . . . if you want to.

*They go in.* WALTER *shuts the door, follows her.*

I'm sorry. Everything's all over the place. I'm at school all day. I don't have much time to tidy up.

*Pause.*

I believe I'm teaching at the school you went to. In the infants.
WALTER: Round the corner? Yes, I went there.

SALLY: You wouldn't believe all the things I've heard about you. You're the apple of your aunts' eyes.

WALTER: So are you.

*Pause.*

SALLY: I'm happy here. I get on very well with them.

WALTER: Look . . . I've got to get something in here . . .

SALLY: In here? I thought you said you'd left something in your room.

WALTER: This is my room.

*Pause.*

SALLY: This?

WALTER: You've taken my room.

SALLY: Have I? I never . . . realized that. Nobody ever told me that. I'm terribly sorry. Do you want it back?

WALTER: I wouldn't mind.

SALLY: Oh dear . . . this is very awkward . . . I must say I'm very comfortable here . . . I mean, where else could I sleep?

WALTER: There's a put-u-up downstairs.

SALLY: Oh, I don't trust those things, do you? I mean, this is such a lovely bed.

WALTER: I know it is. It's mine.

SALLY: You mean I'm sleeping in your bed?

WALTER: Yes.

SALLY: Oh.

*Pause.*

WALTER: I've got something in here I want to get.

SALLY: Well . . . carry on.

WALTER: It's in a rather private place.

SALLY: Do you want me to go out?

WALTER: Yes, if you don't mind.

SALLY: Go out of the room, you mean?

WALTER: It won't take me a minute.
SALLY: What are you looking for?
WALTER: It's a private matter.
SALLY: Is it a gun?

*Pause.*

Can't I turn my back?
WALTER: Two minutes. That's all I want.
SALLY: All right. Two minutes.

*She leaves the room and stands on the landing outside the door.* WALTER *grunts and mutters to himself.*

WALTER: Look at those frills. Frills . . . all over the place. Bloody dolls' house. My damn room.

SALLY'S *voice is heard from the landing.*

SALLY: Are you finished?
WALTER: Just a minute.

*He opens the cupboard and rummages.*

[*Muttering.*] Where's that damn case? Wait a minute . . . what's this?

*Sound of large envelope tearing.*

[*Softly.*] Gaw . . . huuhh!
SALLY: All right?
WALTER: Yes. Thank you.

SALLY *enters the room.*

SALLY: Find it?
WALTER: Yes, thank you.

*He goes to the door.*

What do you teach—ballet?
SALLY: Ballet? No. What a funny question.

WALTER: Not funny. Lots of women teach ballet.
SALLY: I don't dance.

*Pause.*

WALTER: I'm sorry I disturbed your . . . evening.
SALLY: That's all right.
WALTER: Good night.
SALLY: Good night.

*Fade out.*


*Fade in.*

ANNIE: Have another piece of lemon meringue, Mr. Solto.
SOLTO: With pleasure.
ANNIE: You'll like it.
SOLTO: They wanted three hundred and fifty pounds income
tax off me the other day. My word of honour. I said to them,
you must be mad! What are you trying to do, bring me to
an early death? Buy me a cheap spade. I'll get up first thing
in the morning before breakfast and dig my own grave.
Three hundred and fifty-five nicker, eh? I said to them, I
said, show me it, I said show me it down in black and white,
show me where I've earned—must be round about a thousand
pound, you ask me for all that. It's an estimate, they said,
we've estimated your earnings. An estimate? Who did your
*estimate?* A blind man with double vision? I'm an old-age
pensioner. I'm in receipt of three pound a week, find me
something to estimate! What do you say, Walter?
WALTER: They're a lot of villains, the lot of them.
ANNIE: They don't care for the old.
MILLY: Still, you've still got plenty of energy left in you, Mr.
Solto.
SOLTO: Plenty of what?
MILLY: Energy.

SOLTO: Energy? You should have seen me in the outback, in Australia. I was the man who opened up the Northern Territory for them out there.

MILLY: It's a wonder you never got married, Mr. Solto.

SOLTO: I've always been a lone wolf. The first time I was seduced, I said to myself, Solto, watch your step, mind how you go, go so far but no further. If they want to seduce you, let them seduce you, but marry them? Out of the question.

WALTER: Where was that, in Australia or Greece?

SOLTO: Australia.

WALTER: How did you get to Australia from Greece?

SOLTO: By sea. How do you think? I worked my passage. And what a trip. I was only a pubescent. I killed a man with my own hands, a six-foot-ten Lascar from Madagascar.

ANNIE: From Madagascar?

SOLTO: Sure. A Lascar.

MILLY: Alaska?

SOLTO: Madagascar.

*Pause.*

WALTER: It's happened before.

SOLTO: And it'll happen again.

MILLY: Have another piece of swiss roll, Mr. Solto.

ANNIE: I bet you some woman could have made you a good wife.

SOLTO: If I wanted to get married, I could clinch it tomorrow— like that! But I'm like Wally; I'm a lone wolf.

WALTER: How's the scrap business, Mr. Solto?

SOLTO: Ssshh! That's the same question the tax inspector asked me. I told him I retired years ago. He says to me, Why don't you fill out your income tax returns? Why don't you fill out all the forms we send you? I said, I got no income tax to declare, that's why. You're the only man in the district who won't fill out his forms, he says, you want to go to prison? Prison, I said, a man like me, a clean-living old man like me, a man who discovered Don Bradman, it's a national disgrace! Fill out your forms, he says, there'll be no trouble. Listen! I said if you want me to fill out these forms, if you want me to go through all that clerical work, all right, pay me a small sum, pay me for my trouble. Pay me to do it. Otherwise fill them out yourself, leave me alone. Three hundred and fifty-five nicker? They got a fat chance.

ANNIE: A good wife wouldn't have done you no harm. She'd fill out your forms—for you.

SOLTO: That's what I'm afraid of.

MILLY: Have a custard tart, Mr. Solto.

ANNIE: He's still got a good appetite.

SOLTO: I've been saving it up since I last came here.

WALTER: Why, when were you last here, Mr. Solto?

MILLY: It was just after you went inside.

SOLTO: I brought round some daffodils.

ANNIE: Nine months ago, he remembers.

SOLTO: How're they doing?

ANNIE: What?

SOLTO: The daffodils.

ANNIE: Oh, they died.

SOLTO: Go on. [*Eats.*]

WALTER: So you don't know about the lodger?

SOLTO: Lodger?

WALTER: Yes, we've got a lodger now.

MILLY: She's a school teacher.

SOLTO: A school teacher, eh? Hmm. Where does she sleep? On the put-u-up?

WALTER: My aunts gave her my room.

MILLY: Come on, Annie, help me clear the table.

SOLTO: The lady who first seduced me, in Australia—she kicked her own husband out and gave me his room. I bumped into him years later making a speech at Marble Arch. It wasn't a bad speech, it so happens.

MILLY [*stacking plates*]: Why don't you lend Wally a few pound, Mr. Solto?

SOLTO: Me?

ANNIE: Yes, why don't you?

MILLY: You could help to set him up.

SOLTO: Why don't you go to the Prisoners Help Society. They'll give you a loan. I mean, you've done two stretches, you must have a few good references.

WALTER: You wouldn't miss two hundred quid.

SOLTO: Two hundred here, three fifty-five there—what do you think I am, a bank manager?

MILLY: You can't take it with you, Mr. Solto.

WALTER: He wants to be the richest man in the cemetery.

ANNIE: It won't do you much good where you're going, Mr. Solto.

SOLTO: Who's going anywhere?

MILLY: Come on, Annabel.

ANNIE: There's one rock cake left, Mr. Solto.

SOLTO: I'll tell you what, Annie. Keep the rock cake.

MILLY: Annabel.

ANNIE *and* MILLY *go out with plates.*

SOLTO: I wish I could give you a helping hand, Wally. Honest. But things are very tight. I had six cross doubles the other day. Three came home. Number four developed rheumatism at the last hurdle. I went without food for two days.

WALTER: I could do with a lift up. I'm thinking of going straight.

SOLTO: Why? You getting tired of a life of crime?

WALTER: I'm not good enough. I get caught too many times. I'm not clever enough.

SOLTO: You're still on the post-office books?

WALTER: Yes.

SOLTO: It's a mug's game. I've told you before. If you want

to be a forger you've got to have a gift. It's got to come from the heart.

WALTER: I'm not a good enough forger.

SOLTO: You're a terrible forger.

WALTER: That's why I'm always getting caught.

SOLTO: I'm a better forger than you any day. And I don't forge.

WALTER: I haven't got the gift.

SOLTO: A forger's got to love his work. You don't love your work, that's your trouble, Walter.

WALTER: If you lent me two hundred quid I could go straight.

SOLTO: I'm an old-age pensioner, Wally. What are you talking about?

WALTER: If only I could get my room back! I could get settled in, I could think, about things!

SOLTO: Why, who's this school teacher, then? What's the game?

WALTER [*casually*]: Listen, I want to show you something.

SOLTO: What?

WALTER: This photo.

SOLTO: Who's this?

WALTER: A girl . . . I want to find.

SOLTO: Who is she?

WALTER: That's what I want to find out.

SOLTO: We were just talking about forging, about your room, about the school teacher. What's this got to do with it?

WALTER: This is a club, isn't it, in the photo?

SOLTO: Sure.

WALTER: And that girl's a hostess, isn't she?

SOLTO: Sure.

WALTER: Can you locate her?

SOLTO: Me?

*Pause.*

WALTER: Do you know any of these men—these men with her?

SOLTO: O-oh, one of them . . . looks familiar.

WALTER: Find that girl for me. It's important. As a favour. You're the only man I know who could find her. You know these clubs.

SOLTO: Do you know the girl?

*Pause.*

WALTER: No.

SOLTO: Well, where'd you get hold of the photo?

WALTER: I got hold of it.

SOLTO: What have you done? Fallen in love with a photo?

WALTER: Sure. That's right.

SOLTO: Yes . . . A very attractive girl. A lovely girl. All right, Wally. I'll try to find her for you.

WALTER: Thanks.

*Front door slams.*
*Footsteps up the stairs.*

SOLTO: Who's that?

WALTER: That's our lodger. The school teacher.

*Fade out.*


*Fade in.*

MILLY: I don't want the milk hot, I want it cold.

ANNIE: It is cold.

MILLY: I thought you warmed it up.

ANNIE: I did. The time I got up here it's gone cold.

MILLY: You should have kept it in the pan. If you'd brought it up in the pan it would have still been hot.

ANNIE: I thought you said you didn't want it hot.

MILLY: I don't want it hot.

ANNIE: Well, that's why I'm saying it's cold.

MILLY: I know that. But say if I had wanted it hot. That's all I'm saying. [*She sips the milk.*] It could be colder.

ANNIE: Do you want a piece of anchovy or a doughnut?

MILLY: I'll have the anchovy. What are you going to have?

ANNIE: I'm going downstairs, to have a doughnut.

MILLY: You can have this one.

ANNIE: No, I've got one downstairs. You can have it after the anchovy.

MILLY: Why don't you have the anchovy?

ANNIE: You know what I wouldn't mind? I wouldn't mind a few pilchards.

MILLY: Herring. A nice bit of herring, that's what I could do with.

ANNIE: A few pilchards with a drop of vinegar. And a plate of chocolate mousse to go after it.

MILLY: Chocolate mousse?

ANNIE: Don't you remember when we had chocolate mousse at Clacton?

MILLY: Chocolate mousse wouldn't go with herrings.

ANNIE: I'm not having herrings. I'm having pilchards.

*Noise of steps upstairs.*

Listen.

ANNIE *turns the door-handle, listens.*
WALTER *knocks on* SALLY'S *door.*

SALLY: Yes?

WALTER: It's me.

SALLY: Just a moment. Come in.

*Door opens.*

WALTER: How are you?

SALLY: I'm fine.

*Door closes.*

ANNIE: He's in.

MILLY: What do you mean, he's in?

ANNIE: He's gone in.

MILLY: Gone in where, Annie?

ANNIE: Into her room.

MILLY: His room.

ANNIE: His room.

MILLY: He's gone in?

ANNIE: Yes.

MILLY: Is she in there?

ANNIE: Yes.

MILLY: So he's in there with her.

ANNIE: Yes.

MILLY: Go out and have a listen.

> ANNIE *goes out of the door and down the landing to* SALLY'S *door, where she stops.*
> *We hear the following dialogue from her point of view.*

WALTER: Let's have some of this. I've brought it for you.

SALLY: What is it?

WALTER: Brandy.

SALLY: What is this in aid of?

WALTER: Well, I thought we might as well get to know each other, both living in the same house.

SALLY: Yes, why not?

WALTER: Do you drink?

SALLY: Oh, not really.

WALTER: Just one or two now and again, eh?

SALLY: Very occasionally.

WALTER: But you'll have a drop of this?

SALLY: Just a drop . . . Glasses . . .

WALTER: I've got them.

SALLY: All prepared, eh?

> *He opens the bottle and pours.*

WALTER: Cheers.

SALLY: Good health.

WALTER: I wanted to say . . . I was a bit rude yesterday. I wanted to apologize.

SALLY: You weren't rude.

WALTER: It'll just take a bit of getting used to, that's all, you having my room.

SALLY: Well, look, I've been thinking . . . perhaps we could share the room, in—in a kind of way.

WALTER: Share it?

SALLY: I mean, you could use it when I'm not here, or something.

WALTER: Oh, I don't know about that.

SALLY: It'd be quite easy. I'm at school all day.

WALTER: What about the evenings?

SALLY: Well, I'm out three nights a week, you see.

WALTER: Where do you go?

SALLY: Oh, night school. I'm studying languages. Then I usually go on with a girl friend of mine, a history teacher, to listen to some music.

WALTER: What kind of music?

SALLY: Mozart, Brahms. That kind of stuff.

WALTER: Oh, all that kind of stuff.

SALLY: Yes.

*Pause.*

WALTER: Well, it's cosy in here. Have another one.

SALLY: Oh, I . . .

WALTER [*pouring*]: Just one.

SALLY: Thanks. Cheers.

*Pause.*

WALTER: I've never been in this room with a lady before.

SALLY: Oh.

WALTER: The boys used to come here, though. This is where we used to plan our armed robberies.

SALLY: Really?

WALTER: My aunts never told you why I've been inside, have they?

SALLY: No.

WALTER: Well, what it is, you see. I'm a gunman.

SALLY: Oh.

WALTER: Ever met a gunman before?

SALLY: I don't think so.

WALTER: It's not a bad life, all things considered. Plenty of time off. You know, holidays with pay, you could say. No, there's plenty of worse occupations. You're not frightened of me now you know I'm a gunman, are you?

SALLY: No, I think you're charming.

WALTER: Oh, you're right there. That's why I got on so well in prison, you see. Charm. You know what I was doing in there? I was running the prison library. I was the best librarian they ever had. The day I left the Governor gave me a personal send-off. Saw me all the way to the gate. He told me business at the library had shot up out of all recognition since I'd been in charge.

SALLY: What a wonderful compliment.

WALTER [*pouring more drink*]: He told me that if I'd consider giving up armed robbery he'd recommend me for a job in the British Museum. Looking after rare manuscripts. You know, writing my opinion of them.

SALLY: I should think that's quite a skilled job.

WALTER: Cheers. Skilled? Well, funny enough, I've had a good bit to do with rare manuscripts in my time. I used to know a bloke who ran a business digging them up.

SALLY: Digging what up?

WALTER: Rare manuscripts. Out of tombs. I used to give him a helping hand when I was on the loose. Very well paid it was, too. You see, they were nearly always attached to a corpse, these manuscripts, you had to lift up the pelvis bone with a pair of tweezers. Big tweezers. Can't leave fingerprints on a corpse, you see. Canon law. The biggest shock I ever had was when a skeleton collapsed on top of me and nearly bit my ear off. I had a funny feeling at that moment. I thought I was the skeleton and he was my long-lost uncle come to kiss me good night. You've never been inside a grave, I suppose. I can recommend it, honest, I mean if you want to taste everything life has to offer.

SALLY: Well, I'll be inside one, one day.

WALTER: Oh, I don't know. You might be cremated, or drowned at sea, mightn't you?

ANNIE *creeps back down the landing into the* AUNTS' *room and gets into bed.*

MILLY: Did you listen?

ANNIE: Yes.

MILLY: Well?

ANNIE: I heard them talking.

MILLY: What were they saying?

ANNIE: Don't ask me.

MILLY: Go to the door again. Listen properly.

ANNIE: Why don't you go.

MILLY: I'm in bed.

ANNIE: So am I.

MILLY: But I've been in bed longer than you.

ANNIE *mutters and grumbles to herself, gets out of bed and goes back along the landing to the door. The dialogue heard is still from her point of view.*

WALTER: You're a Northerner?

SALLY: That's clever of you. I thought I'd . . .

WALTER: I can tell the accent.

SALLY: I thought I'd lost it . . .

WALTER: There's something in your eyes too. You only find it in Lancashire girls.

SALLY: Really? What?

WALTER [*moving closer*]: You seem a bit uncomfortable with me. Why's that?

SALLY: I'm not uncomfortable.

WALTER: Why's that, then? You seem a bit uneasy.

SALLY: I'm not.

WALTER: Let's fill you up, eh? I mean you were different yesterday. You were on top of yourself yesterday.

SALLY: It's you who were different. You're different today.

WALTER: You don't want to worry about me being an armed robber. They call me the gentle gunman.

SALLY: I'm not worried.

*Pause.*

WALTER: My aunties think you're marvellous. I think they've got us in mind for the marriage stakes.

SALLY: What?

WALTER: Yes, I think they think they've found me a wife.

SALLY: How funny.

WALTER: They've roped you in to take part in a wedding. They've forgotten one thing, though.

SALLY: What's that?

WALTER: I'm married. As a matter of fact, I'm married to three women. I'm a triple bigamist. Do you believe me?

SALLY: I think you're in a very strange mood.

WALTER: It's the look in your eyes that's brought it on.

SALLY: You haven't got such bad eyes yourself.

WALTER: Your eyes, they're Northern eyes. They're full of soot.

SALLY: Thank you.

WALTER [*pouring*]: Top it up. Come on.

SALLY: To our eyes.

WALTER: I thought you didn't drink. You can knock it back

all right. Keep in practice in school, I suppose. In the milk break. Keeps you in trim for netball. Or at that night school, eh? I bet you enjoy yourself there. Come on. Tell me what you get up to at that night school.

ANNIE *yawns slightly and pads back to her room. She closes door and gets into bed.*

ANNIE: Still talking.
MILLY: What are they talking about? [*Sleepily.*]
ANNIE: I can't make it out.
MILLY: I should have gone. You're as deaf as a post.

*They settle in bed. Squeaks.*

ANNIE: The doughnut's given me heartburn. [*Faintly.*] Good night.

MILLY *snores briefly.*
*Fade into* SALLY'S *room.*

SALLY: I lead a quiet life, a very quiet life, I don't mix with people.
WALTER: Except me. You're mixing with me.
SALLY: I don't have any kind of social life.
WALTER: I'll have to take you round a few of the clubs I know, show you the sights.
SALLY: No, I don't like that.
WALTER: What do you like?

*Pause.*

SALLY: Lying here . . . by myself . . .
WALTER: On my bed.
SALLY: Yes.
WALTER: Doing what?
SALLY: Thinking.
WALTER: Think about me last night?
SALLY: You?

WALTER: This offer to share your room, I might consider it.

*Pause.*

I bet you're thinking about me now.

*Pause.*

SALLY: Why should I be?
WALTER: I'm thinking about you.

*Pause.*

I don't know why I made such a fuss about this room. It's just an ordinary room, there's nothing to it. I mean if you weren't here. If you weren't in it, there'd be nothing to it.

*Pause.*

Why don't you stay in it? It's not true that I'm married. I just said that. I'm not attached. To tell you the truth . . . to tell you the truth, I'm still looking for Miss Right.
SALLY: I think I should move away from here.
WALTER: Where would you go?

*Pause.*

SALLY: Anywhere.
WALTER: Would you go to the seaside? I could come with you. We could do a bit of fishing . . . on the pier. Yes, we could go together. Or, on the other hand, we could stay here. We could stay where we are.
SALLY: Could we?
WALTER: Sit down.
SALLY: What?
WALTER: Sit down. [*Pause.*] Cross your legs.
SALLY: Mmmmm?
WALTER: Cross your legs.

*Pause.*

Uncross them.

*Pause.*

Stand up.

*Pause.*

Turn round.

*Pause.*

Stop.

*Pause.*

Sit down.

*Pause.*

Cross your legs.

*Pause.*

Uncross your legs.

*Silence.*


*Night-club music.*

TULLY: No, I tell you, it must be . . . wait a minute, must be round about ten years. The last time was when I was down at Richmond.

SOLTO: Yes, the Donkey Club.

TULLY: The Donkey, sure. I left there three years ago.

SOLTO: How long you been here, then? I haven't been down here for about three years.

TULLY: You must have missed me. I come here three years ago, that's exactly when I come here. [*Calls.*] Charlie!

TULLY *clicks his fingers for the* WAITER.

SOLTO: It was a real dive before then, I can tell you.

WAITER: Same again, Mr. Tully?

TULLY: Same again. Dive—course it was a dive. They asked me to come here and give it—you know—a bit of class, about three years ago. I gave the boot to about a dozen lowlives from the start, you know, I made my position clear.

SOLTO: Didn't they give you no trouble?

TULLY: With me? Listen, they know if they want to start making trouble they picked the right customer. Don't you remember me at Blackheath.

SOLTO: You're going back a bit.

TULLY: I'm going back a few years before the war.

SOLTO: You're going back to when the game was good.

TULLY: What about you at Blackheath?

SOLTO: Blackheath. It's another story when you start talking about Blackheath.

TULLY: Thanks, Charlie. Here you are, Ambrose. Cheers.

*Pause.*

No, you can see it's not a dive no more. I got the place moving, I mean, we got a band up there—well, I say a band —a piano and a double bass, but they're very good boys, they're good boys. We got a very nice clientele come in here. You know, you get a lot of musicians . . . er . . . musicians coming down here. They make up a very nice clientele. Of course, you get a certain amount of business executives. I mean, high-class people. I was talking to a few of them only the other night. They come over from Hampton Court, they come, from Twickenham, from Datchet.

SOLTO: All the way from Datchet?

TULLY: Sure, they get in the car, how long's it taken them? They come here for a bit of relaxation. I mean, we got a two-o'clock licence. We got three resident birds. What made you come down here all of a sudden?

SOLTO: Ah, just one of them funny things, Cyril. I heard of a little bird.

TULLY: What, one of the birds here?

SOLTO: Still sharp, eh, Cyril?

TULLY: You heard about the quality we got here, eh? We got some high-class dolls down here, don't worry. They come all the way from finishing school.

*Fade out.*


*Fade in: girls' dressing-room.*

BARBARA: What did he say then?

SALLY: Come over with me one Sunday, he says, come over and have Sunday dinner, meet the wife. Why, I said, what are you going to introduce me as, your sister? No, he says; she's very broad-minded, my wife; she'll be delighted to meet you.

MAVIS: Oh yes, I've heard of that kind of thing before.

SALLY: Yes, that's what I said. Oh yes, I said, I've heard of that kind of thing before. Go on, get off out of it, I said, buzz off before I call a copper.

BARBARA: Which was he, the one with the big nose?

SALLY: Yes.

MANAGER: Come on, girls, move yourselves, we're ready for the off.

BARBARA: Who asked you to come into the ladies' room?

MANAGER: Don't give me no lip. Get your skates on. [*To* SALLY:] Cyril wants you at his table right away.

SALLY: I'll kick him in the middle of his paraphernalia one of these days.

BARBARA: Go on, what happened then?

SALLY: Why don't you come on the river with me one of these days? he says. I'll take you for a ride in a punt.

MAVIS: In a what?

BARBARA: A punt.

MAVIS: What's a punt?

SALLY: I said to him, In a punt, with you? You must be mad. You won't get me in no punt.

BARBARA: I thought you said he attracted you.

SALLY: Oh, he did to start off, that's all. I thought he wasn't bad. But, you know, he came from Australia. He'd got a lot of Australian habits, they didn't go down very well with me.

MANAGER: Come on, come on, I don't want to tell you again. Where do you think you are, on Brighton front? [*To* SALLY:] Cyril wants you at his table.

SALLY: I'll cut his ears off one of these days.

*She goes into the club.*

SOLTO: So I thought to myself, Tully, Big Johnny Bolsom. She must be all right.

TULLY: Sure she's all right.

SOLTO: So I thought I'd follow it up.

TULLY: You couldn't have done better. Here she is, here she is, come on, darling. This is an old friend of mine, Ambrose Solto.

SOLTO: How do you do?

SALLY: How do you do?

TULLY: Sit down, Ambrose. I want you to meet this girl, Ambrose. This is the cleverest girl we got here. She speaks three languages.

SOLTO: What languages?

TULLY: Tell him.

SALLY: Well, English for a start.

SOLTO: She's witty too, eh?

TULLY: Witty? She's my favourite girl.

SALLY: Oh, I'm not.

SOLTO: Aren't you going to tell me your name?

SALLY: Katina.

SOLTO: Katina. What a coincidence! My childhood sweetheart was called Katina.

TULLY: No. Go on!

SALLY: Really, Mr. Solto?

SOLTO: Yes, when I was a little boy, when I was a little boy in Athens. That's when it was.

*Fade out.*

*Fade in.*

WALTER: I just took the train down to Southend, that's all.

ANNIE: Southend? What for?

WALTER: I felt like having a look at the seaside. It wasn't bad down there. I rolled around, that's all. Smelt the old sea, that's all.

*Pause.*

ANNIE: You've got a secret.

WALTER: Have I?

ANNIE: Oh, come on, Wally, what do you think of her? She's nice, isn't she?

WALTER: Who, the girl upstairs? Yes, she's a very nice girl.

ANNIE: You like her, eh?

WALTER: Who?

ANNIE: Don't you?

WALTER: What, the one that lives upstairs, eh?

ANNIE: All larking aside.

WALTER: Well . . . all larking aside . . . without any larking . . . I'd say she was all right.

ANNIE: You didn't like her, though, the first going off, did you?

WALTER: Ah well, the first going off . . . ain't anything like . . . the second going off, is it? What I mean to say . . . is that the second going off . . . often turns out to be very different . . . from what you thought it was going to be . . . on the first going off. If you see what I'm saying.

ANNIE: Hasn't she made the room lovely, eh?

WALTER: Very snazzy.

ANNIE: She's made it really feminine, hasn't she?

WALTER: Oh . . . without a shadow of doubt.

ANNIE: She should be in soon. She should be due home from night school in about half an hour.

*Fade out and in: Night club.*

SOLTO: What do you think of that?

SALLY: No, you've got real rhythm. Mr. Solto, it's a pleasure.

SOLTO: I've always had rhythm. Take it from me. I was born with rhythm. My big toe can dance a polka by himself. My word of honour. My sweetheart and me, we used to dance by the sea at night, with the waves coming in. You ever done that?

SALLY: No. Never. Let's have a drink.

TULLY: How you getting on, you two?

SOLTO: Marvellous.

SALLY: Lovely.

SOLTO: See us on the floor?

TULLY: What were you doing on the floor?

SALLY: Dancing!

SOLTO: You should have seen him at Blackheath. Go on, off you go, Cyril, we're talking about philosophy here.

TULLY: Mind how you go.

*He goes.*
SOLTO *and* SALLY *go to the table and sit.*

SOLTO: I was going to say something to you.

SALLY: What?

SOLTO: I own a private beach. On the South Coast. It's all my own. A little beach hut. Well, not so little. It's big. It's not a hut either. It's a bit bigger than a hut. It's got Indian carpets, it's got the front side full of windows looking out to the sea, it's got central heating, and the waves . . . the waves come right up to the front step. You can lie on a divan and watch them come closer and closer. How would you like to lie there in the moonlight, eh, and watch the waves come closer and closer?

SALLY: Sounds . . . very nice.

SOLTO: Next week-end we'll go down, eh?

SALLY: Well, I . . .

SOLTO: No excuses! I'll barbecue a boar on the beach, my word of honour.

SALLY: Where you going to get the boar?

SOLTO: Specially from France—where else? Listen. You want to know a little secret? I came down here specifically to look for you.

SALLY: What do you mean?

SOLTO: I got hold of this photo of you, see? So I got hold of the photographer. He told me what club it was, and here I am.

SALLY: Where'd you get the photo?

SOLTO: That I'm not supposed to tell you. You see, what I was doing, I was looking for you for a pal of mine.

SALLY: A pal? . . . Who?

SOLTO: Don't worry about it. I'm not going to tell him where he can find you. No. I wouldn't let a man like that get hold of a lovely girl like you.

SALLY: What's his name?

SOLTO: He's a man called Wally. Wally Street. He's always in and out of the nick. He's a forger, a petty thief, does post-office books. You know him?

SALLY: No.

SOLTO: Funny . . . I don't know what he . . . anyway, forget all about it. But I'll give him his due. If it wasn't for him showing me this photo, where would I be, eh. And where would you be.

SALLY: Yes. Where would I be?

*Fade out and in.*
*A knock at the front door.*
WALTER *goes through the hall door.*

SOLTO: Hullo, Wally, I'll come in a minute. I've got a cab outside.

*They go into the room.*

WALTER: What's up? Have you found the girl?
SOLTO: The girl? What girl?
WALTER: The girl. That photo I gave you. You know.
SOLTO: Oh, the girl! You mean the girl I was trying to . . .
WALTER: Yes, I thought that might be why you've come round.
SOLTO: You're dead right. That's exactly why I've come round.
WALTER: That's what I thought.
SOLTO: And you weren't wrong.

*Pause.*

WALTER: Well. Where is she?
SOLTO: That's what I wanted to tell you. I can't find her.
WALTER: You can't find her?
SOLTO: Not a smell. That's exactly what I came round to tell you.
WALTER: Not a smell, eh.
SOLTO: Not a whiff.
WALTER: I thought you were on her track.
SOLTO: There's no track. I been everywhere. The Madrigal. The Whip Room. The Gamut. Pedros. Nobody knew the face. Wait a minute—Pedro said he might have seen her once round a few back doubles in Madrid. She been to Madrid?
WALTER: How would I know? I've never met her.
SOLTO: I thought you had.
WALTER: Didn't you locate that club?

SOLTO: What club?

WALTER: In the photo.

SOLTO: No. What I thought, the best thing to do would be to get hold of the photographer, you see. So I paid him a call.

WALTER: What did he say?

SOLTO: He wasn't there. He'd gone to Canada for a conference.

WALTER: What kind of conference?

SOLTO: A dental conference. He's going to be a dentist.

WALTER: Why'd he give up photography?

SOLTO: He had a change of heart. You know how it is. He gave me a cup of coffee, told me his life story.

WALTER: Who did?

SOLTO: His brother. The chiropodist. He's in dead trouble that boy, he can't meet his overheads.

WALTER: Look here, Mr. Solto, if I were you, I'd give up the whole thing.

SOLTO: You want my opinion? I think the photo's a fake. There's no such club. There's no girl. They don't exist.

WALTER: That's exactly what I think.

*Pause.*

SOLTO: You do?

WALTER: Exactly.

SOLTO: Who knows? You might be right.

WALTER: That photo. It's a fake. You'll never find her.

SOLTO: How can it be a fake? I thought you knew her.

WALTER: I never said I knew her. I've never met her.

SOLTO: But that's what I'm saying. There's no one to know. You've never seen her. I've never seen her. There's no one to see.

WALTER: She doesn't exist.

*Pause.*

SOLTO: All the same, look, the girl's there. That's the photo of someone.

WALTER: No one I know.

*Pause.*

SOLTO: Take my tip, Wally, wipe the whole business from your head, wipe it clean out of your mind.

WALTER: That's what I think you'd better do, Mr. Solto.

*Front door. Footsteps.*

SOLTO: What's that?

WALTER: That's the school teacher.

SOLTO: That's your mark. Someone with an education. She keeps nice hours for a school teacher. Where's she been, night school?

*Fade out and in to footsteps on stairs.*
*Knock on the door.*

WALTER: Are you there?

*He tries the door. It is locked.*

Are you in there? I want to speak to you. Let me in a minute. Will you let me in a minute? What's up with you? What the hell's up with you? Let me in. I want to speak to you.

*Silence.*

ANNIE: She's gone.

MILLY: Gone?

ANNIE: Here's a note.

MILLY: Where's she gone?

ANNIE: She left a note.

MILLY: What does it say?

ANNIE: Dear Misses Billet. I'm very sorry, but an urgent matter has called me away suddenly. I don't know when I'll be back, so I thought I better take everything. I didn't want to wake you up. Thank you. Good-bye. Sally. I'm going to tell Wally.

ANNIE'S *footsteps into the front room.*

Wally. Wake up.

*Pause.*

She's gone away.

WALTER: Who?

ANNIE: She left a note. Look.

*Pause while he reads.*

WALTER: Yes, well . . . she . . . obviously had to go away.

*Pause.*

ANNIE: You didn't have any arguments with her, did you, Wally?

WALTER: No.

ANNIE: You didn't see her last night after she came back from night school?

WALTER: No.

MILLY *enters.*

MILLY: I just found this photo in her room.

ANNIE: Ah. Doesn't she look lovely holding that netball?

MILLY: With all the schoolgirls.

ANNIE: I never knew she was the games mistress. She never told us.

*Pause.*

MILLY: It looks as though she's gone for good.

*Pause.*

WALTER: Yes.

*Pause.*

That's what it looks like.

*Fade.*

# REVUE SKETCHES

*Last to Go* and *Request Stop* were performed in the revue *Pieces of Eight* at the Apollo Theatre, London, in 1959.

*The Black and White* and *Trouble in the Works* were performed in the revue *One to Another* at the Lyric Opera House, Hammersmith, and at the Apollo Theatre, London, in 1959.

# TROUBLE IN THE WORKS

*An office in a factory.* MR. FIBBS *at the desk. A knock at the door. Enter* MR. WILLS.

FIBBS: Ah, Wills. Good. Come in. Sit down, will you?
WILLS: Thanks, Mr. Fibbs.
FIBBS: You got my message?
WILLS: I just got it.
FIBBS: Good. Good.

*Pause.*

Good. Well now . . . Have a cigar?
WILLS: No, thanks, not for me, Mr. Fibbs.
FIBBS: Well, now, Wills, I hear there's been a little trouble in the factory.
WILLS: Yes, I . . . I suppose you could call it that, Mr. Fibbs.
FIBBS: Well, what in heaven's name is it all about?
WILLS: Well, I don't exactly know how to put it, Mr. Fibbs.
FIBBS: Now come on, Wills, I've got to know what it is, before I can do anything about it.
WILLS: Well, Mr. Fibbs, it's simply a matter that the men have . . . well, they seem to have taken a turn against some of the products.
FIBBS: Taken a turn?
WILLS: They just don't seem to like them much any more.
FIBBS: Don't like them? But we've got the reputation of having the finest machine part turnover in the country. They're the best paid men in the industry. We've got the cheapest canteen in Yorkshire. No two menus are alike. We've got a billiard hall, haven't we, on the premises, we've got a swimming pool for use of staff. And what about the long-playing record room? And you tell me they're dissatisfied?

WILLS: Oh, the men are very grateful for all the amenities, sir. They just don't like the products.

FIBBS: But they're beautiful products. I've been in the business a lifetime. I've never seen such beautiful products.

WILLS: There it is, sir.

FIBBS: Which ones don't they like?

WILLS: Well, there's the brass pet cock, for instance.

FIBBS: The brass pet cock? What's the matter with the brass pet cock?

WILLS: They just don't seem to like it any more.

FIBBS: But what exactly don't they like about it?

WILLS: Perhaps it's just the look of it.

FIBBS: That brass pet cock? But I tell you it's perfection. Nothing short of perfection.

WILLS: They've just gone right off it.

FIBBS: Well, I'm flabbergasted.

WILLS: It's not only the brass pet cock, Mr. Fibbs.

FIBBS: What else?

WILLS: There's the hemi unibal spherical rod end.

FIBBS: The hemi unibal spherical rod end? Where could you find a finer rod end?

WILLS: There are rod ends and rod ends, Mr. Fibbs.

FIBBS: I know there are rod ends and rod ends. But where could you find a finer hemi unibal spherical rod end?

WILLS: They just don't want to have anything more to do with it.

FIBBS: This is shattering. Shattering. What else? Come on, Wills. There's no point in hiding anything from me.

WILLS: Well, I hate to say it, but they've gone very vicious about the high speed taper shank spiral flute reamers.

FIBBS: The high speed taper shank spiral flute reamers! But that's absolutely ridiculous! What could they possibly have against the high speed taper shank spiral flute reamers?

WILLS: All I can say is they're in a state of very bad agitation about them. And then there's the gunmetal side outlet relief with handwheel.

FIBBS: What!

WILLS: There's the nippled connector and the nippled adaptor and the vertical mechanical comparator.

FIBBS: No!

WILLS: And the one they can't speak about without trembling is the jaw for Jacob's chuck for use on portable drill.

FIBBS: My own Jacob's chuck? Not my very own Jacob's chuck?

WILLS: They've just taken a turn against the whole lot of them, I tell you. Male elbow adaptors, tubing nuts, grub screws, internal fan washers, dog points, half dog points, white metal bushes—

FIBBS: But not, surely not, my lovely parallel male stud couplings.

WILLS: They hate and detest your lovely parallel male stud couplings, and the straight flange pump connectors, and back nuts, and front nuts, *and* the bronzedraw off cock with handwheel and the bronzedraw off cock without handwheel!

FIBBS: Not the bronzedraw off cock with handwheel?

WILLS: And without handwheel.

FIBBS: Without handwheel?

WILLS: And with handwheel.

FIBBS: Not with handwheel?

WILLS: And without handwheel.

FIBBS: Without handwheel?

WILLS: With handwheel *and* without handwheel.

FIBBS: With handwheel *and* without handwheel?

WILLS: With or without!

*Pause.*

FIBBS [*broken*]: Tell me. What do they want to make in its place?

WILLS: Brandy balls.

# THE BLACK AND WHITE

*The* FIRST OLD WOMAN *is sitting at a milk bar table. Small.*
*A* SECOND OLD WOMAN *approaches. Tall. She is carrying two*
*bowls of soup, which are covered by two plates, on each of*
*which is a slice of bread. She puts the bowls down on the*
*table carefully.*

SECOND: You see that one come up and speak to me at the
counter?

*She takes the bread plates off the bowls, takes two spoons*
*from her pocket, and places the bowls, plates and spoons.*

FIRST: You got the bread, then?
SECOND: I didn't know how I was going to carry it. In the end
I put the plates on top of the soup.
FIRST: I like a bit of bread with my soup.

*They begin the soup. Pause.*

SECOND: Did you see that one come up and speak to me at
the counter?
FIRST: Who?
SECOND: Comes up to me, he says, hullo, he says, what's the
time by your clock? Bloody liberty. I was just standing
there getting your soup.
FIRST: It's tomato soup.
SECOND: What's the time by your clock? he says.
FIRST: I bet you answered him back.
SECOND: I told him all right. Go on, I said, why don't you
get back into your scraghole, I said, clear off out of it before
I call a copper.

*Pause.*

FIRST: I not long got here.

SECOND: Did you get the all-night bus?

FIRST: I got the all-night bus straight here.

SECOND: Where from?

FIRST: Marble Arch.

SECOND: Which one?

FIRST: The two-nine-four, that takes me all the way to Fleet Street.

SECOND: So does the two-nine-one. [*Pause.*] I see you talking to two strangers as I come in. You want to stop talking to strangers, old piece of boot like you, you mind who you talk to.

FIRST: I wasn't talking to any strangers.

*Pause. The* FIRST OLD WOMAN *follows the progress of a bus through the window.*

That's another all-night bus gone down. [*Pause.*] Going up the other way. Fulham way. [*Pause.*] That was a two-nine-seven. [*Pause.*] I've never been up that way. [*Pause.*] I've been down to Liverpool Street.

SECOND: That's up the other way.

FIRST: I don't fancy going down there, down Fulham way, and all up there.

SECOND: Uh-uh.

FIRST: I've never fancied that direction much.

*Pause.*

SECOND: How's your bread?

*Pause.*

FIRST: Eh?

SECOND: Your bread.

FIRST: All right. How's yours?

*Pause.*

SECOND: They don't charge for the bread if you have soup.

FIRST: They do if you have tea.

SECOND: If you have tea they do. [*Pause.*] You talk to strangers they'll take you in. Mind my word. Coppers'll take you in.

FIRST: I don't talk to strangers.

SECOND: They took me away in the wagon once.

FIRST: They didn't keep you though.

SECOND: They didn't keep me, but that was only because they took a fancy to me. They took a fancy to me when they got me in the wagon.

FIRST: Do you think they'd take a fancy to me?

SECOND: I wouldn't back on it.

*The* FIRST OLD WOMAN *gazes out of the window.*

FIRST: You can see what goes on from this top table. [*Pause.*] It's better than going down to that place on the embankment, anyway.

SECOND: Yes, there's not too much noise.

FIRST: There's always a bit of noise.

SECOND: Yes, there's always a bit of life.

*Pause.*

FIRST: They'll be closing down soon to give it a scrub-round.

SECOND: There's a wind out.

*Pause.*

FIRST: I wouldn't mind staying.

SECOND: They won't let you.

FIRST: I know. [*Pause.*] Still, they only close hour and half, don't they? [*Pause.*] It's not long. [*Pause.*] You can go along, then come back.

SECOND: I'm going. I'm not coming back.

FIRST: When it's light I come back. Have my tea.

SECOND: I'm going. I'm going up to the Garden.

FIRST: I'm not going down there. [*Pause.*] I'm going up to Waterloo Bridge.

SECOND: You'll just about see the last two-nine-six come up
    over the river.

FIRST: I'll just catch a look of it. Time I get up there.

*Pause.*

It don't look like an all-night bus in daylight, do it?


# REQUEST STOP

*A queue at a Request Bus Stop. A* WOMAN *at the head, with a*
SMALL MAN *in a raincoat next to her, two other* WOMEN *and
a* MAN.

WOMAN [*to* SMALL MAN]: I beg your pardon, what did you say?

*Pause.*

All I asked you was if I could get a bus from here to Shepherds Bush.

*Pause.*

Nobody asked you to start making insinuations.

*Pause.*

Who do you think you are?

*Pause.*

Huh. I know your sort, I know your type. Don't worry,
I know all about people like you.

*Pause.*

We can all tell where you come from. They're putting
your sort inside every day of the week.

*Pause.*

All I've got to do, is report you, and you'd be standing in the dock in next to no time. One of my best friends is a plain clothes detective.

*Pause.*

I know all about it. Standing there as if butter wouldn't melt in your mouth. Meet you in a dark alley it'd be . . . another story. [*To the others, who stare into space.*] You heard what this man said to me. All I asked him was if I could get a bus from here to Shepherds Bush. [*To him.*] I've got witnesses, don't you worry about that.

*Pause.*

Impertinence.

*Pause.*

Ask a man a civil question he treats you like a threepenny bit. [*To him.*] I've got better things to do, my lad, I can assure you. I'm not going to stand here and be insulted on a public highway. Anyone can tell you're a foreigner. I was born just around the corner. Anyone can tell you're just up from the country for a bit of a lark. I know your sort.

*Pause.*

*She goes to a* LADY.

Excuse me lady. I'm thinking of taking this man up to the magistrate's court, you heard him make that crack, would you like to be a witness?

*The* LADY *steps into the road.*

LADY: Taxi . . .

*She disappears.*

WOMAN: We know what sort she is. [*Back to position.*] I was the first in this queue.

*Pause.*

Born just round the corner. Born and bred. These people from the country haven't the faintest idea of how to behave. Peruvians. You're bloody lucky I don't put you on a charge. You ask a straightforward question—

*The others suddenly thrust out their arms at a passing bus. They run off left after it. The* WOMAN, *alone, clicks her teeth and mutters. A man walks from the right to the stop, and waits. She looks at him out of the corner of her eye. At length she speaks shyly, hesitantly, with a slight smile.*

Excuse me. Do you know if I can get a bus from here . . . to Marble Arch?


# LAST TO GO

*A coffee stall. A* BARMAN *and an old* NEWSPAPER SELLER. *The* BARMAN *leans on his counter, the* OLD MAN *stands with tea. Silence.*

MAN: You was a bit busier earlier.
BARMAN: Ah.
MAN: Round about ten.
BARMAN: Ten, was it?
MAN: About then.

*Pause.*

I passed by here about then.
BARMAN: Oh yes?
MAN: I noticed you were doing a bit of trade.

*Pause.*

BARMAN: Yes, trade was very brisk here about ten.
MAN: Yes, I noticed.

*Pause.*

I sold my last one about then. Yes. About nine forty-five.
BARMAN: Sold your last then, did you?
MAN: Yes, my last 'Evening News' it was. Went about twenty
to ten.

*Pause.*

BARMAN: 'Evening News', was it?
MAN: Yes.

*Pause.*

Sometimes it's the 'Star' is the last to go.
BARMAN: Ah.
MAN: Or the . . . whatsisname.
BARMAN: 'Standard'.
MAN: Yes.

*Pause.*

All I had left tonight was the 'Evening News'.

*Pause.*

BARMAN: Then that went, did it?
MAN: Yes.

*Pause.*

Like a shot.

*Pause.*

BARMAN: You didn't have any left, eh?

MAN: No. Not after I sold that one.

*Pause.*

BARMAN: It was after that you must have come by here then, was it?

MAN: Yes, I come by here after that, see, after I packed up.

BARMAN: You didn't stop here though, did you?

MAN: When?

BARMAN: I mean, you didn't stop here and have a cup of tea then, did you?

MAN: What, about ten?

BARMAN: Yes.

MAN: No, I went up to Victoria.

BARMAN: No, I thought I didn't see you.

MAN: I had to go up to Victoria.

*Pause.*

BARMAN: Yes, trade was very brisk here about then.

*Pause.*

MAN: I went to see if I could get hold of George.

BARMAN: Who?

MAN: George.

*Pause.*

BARMAN: George who?

MAN: George . . . whatsisname.

BARMAN: Oh.

*Pause.*

Did you get hold of him?

MAN: No. No, I couldn't get hold of him. I couldn't locate him.

BARMAN: He's not about much now, is he?

*Pause.*

MAN: When did you last see him then?

BARMAN: Oh, I haven't seen him for years.

S.A.–I

MAN: No, nor me.

*Pause.*

BARMAN: Used to suffer very bad from arthritis.
MAN: Arthritis?
BARMAN: Yes.
MAN: He never suffered from arthritis.
BARMAN: Suffered very bad.

*Pause.*

MAN: Not when I knew him.

*Pause.*

BARMAN: I think he must have left the area.

*Pause.*

MAN: Yes, it was the 'Evening News' was the last to go tonight.
BARMAN: Not always the last though, is it, though?
MAN: No. Oh no. I mean sometimes it's the 'News'. Other times it's one of the others. No way of telling beforehand. Until you've got your last one left, of course. Then you can tell which one it's going to be.
BARMAN: Yes.

*Pause.*

MAN: Oh yes.

*Pause.*

I think he must have left the area.

# APPLICANT

*An office.* LAMB, *a young man, eager, cheerful, enthusiastic, is striding nervously, alone. The door opens.* MISS PIFFS *comes in. She is the essence of efficiency.*

PIFFS: Ah, good morning.

LAMB: Oh, good morning, miss.

PIFFS: Are you Mr. Lamb?

LAMB: That's right.

PIFFS [*studying a sheet of paper*]: Yes. You're applying for this vacant post, aren't you?

LAMB: I am actually, yes.

PIFFS: Are you a physicist?

LAMB: Oh yes, indeed. It's my whole life.

PIFFS [*languidly*]: Good. Now our procedure is, that before we discuss the applicant's qualifications we like to subject him to a little test to determine his psychological suitability. You've no objection?

LAMB: Oh, good heavens, no.

PIFFS: Jolly good.

MISS PIFFS *has taken some objects out of a drawer and goes to* LAMB. *She places a chair for him.*

PIFFS: Please sit down. [*He sits.*] Can I fit these to your palms?

LAMB [*affably*]: What are they?

PIFFS: Electrodes.

LAMB: Oh yes, of course. Funny little things.

*She attaches them to his palms.*

PIFFS: Now the earphones.

*She attaches earphones to his head.*

LAMB: I say how amusing.
PIFFS: Now I plug in.

*She plugs in to the wall.*

LAMB [*a trifle nervously*]: Plug in, do you? Oh yes, of course.
Yes, you'd have to, wouldn't you?

MISS PIFFS *perches on a high stool and looks down on* LAMB.

This help to determine my . . . my suitability does it?
PIFFS: Unquestionably. Now relax. Just relax. Don't think
about a thing.
LAMB: No.
PIFFS: Relax completely. Rela-a-a-x. Quite relaxed?

LAMB *nods.* MISS PIFFS *presses a button on the side of her
stool. A piercing high pitched buzz-hum is heard.* LAMB *jolts
rigid. His hands go to his earphones. He is propelled from the
chair. He tries to crawl under the chair.* MISS PIFFS *watches,
impassive. The noise stops.* LAMB *peeps out from under the
chair, crawls out, stands, twitches, emits a short chuckle and
collapses in the chair.*

PIFFS: Would you say you were an excitable person?
LAMB: Not—not unduly, no. Of course, I—
PIFFS: Would you say you were a moody person?
LAMB: Moody? No, I wouldn't say I was moody—well,
sometimes occasionally I—
PIFFS: Do you ever get fits of depression?
LAMB: Well, I wouldn't call them depression exactly—
PIFFS: Do you often do things you regret in the morning?
LAMB: Regret? Things I regret? Well, it depends what you
mean by often, really—I mean when you say often—
PIFFS: Are you often puzzled by women?
LAMB: Women?
PIFFS: Men.

LAMB: Men? Well, I was just going to answer the question about women—

PIFFS: Do you often feel puzzled?

LAMB: Puzzled?

PIFFS: By women.

LAMB: Women?

PIFFS: Men.

LAMB: Oh, now just a minute, I . . . Look, do you want separate answers or a joint answer?

PIFFS: After your day's work do you ever feel tired? Edgy? Fretty? Irritable? At a loose end? Morose? Frustrated? Morbid? Unable to concentrate? Unable to sleep? Unable to eat? Unable to remain seated? Unable to remain upright? Lustful? Indolent? On heat? Randy? Full of desire? Full of energy? Full of dread? Drained? of energy, of dread? of desire?

*Pause.*

LAMB [*thinking*]: Well, it's difficult to say really . . .

PIFFS: Are you a good mixer?

LAMB: Well, you've touched on quite an interesting point there—

PIFFS: Do you suffer from eczema, listlessness, or falling coat?

LAMB: Er . . .

PIFFS: Are you virgo intacta?

LAMB: I beg your pardon?

PIFFS: Are you virgo intacta?

LAMB: Oh, I say, that's rather embarrassing. I mean—in front of a lady—

PIFFS: Are you virgo intacta?

LAMB: Yes, I am, actually. I'll make no secret of it.

PIFFS: Have you always been virgo intacta?

LAMB: Oh yes, always. Always.

PIFFS: From the word go?

LAMB: Go? Oh yes, from the word go.

PIFFS: Do women frighten you?

*She presses a button on the other side of her stool. The stage is plunged into redness, which flashes on and off in time with her questions.*

PIFFS [*building*]: Their clothes? Their shoes? Their voices? Their laughter? Their stares? Their way of walking? Their way of sitting? Their way of smiling? Their way of talking? Their mouths? Their hands? Their feet? Their shins? Their thighs? Their knees? Their eyes?
Their [*Drumbeat*]. Their [*Drumbeat*]. Their [*Cymbal bang*]. Their [*Trombone chord*]. Their [*Bass note*].

LAMB [*in a high voice*]. Well it depends what you mean really—

*The light still flashes. She presses the other button and the piercing buzz-hum is heard again.* LAMB'S *hands go to his earphones. He is propelled from the chair, falls, rolls, crawls, totters and collapses.*

*Silence.*

*He lies face upwards.* MISS PIFFS *looks at him then walks to* LAMB *and bends over him.*

PIFFS: Thank you very much, Mr. Lamb. We'll let you know.